"Sensible, readable and immediately implementable

Author of *Your Erroneou*   *agic*

"A road map filled with easy to follow spiritual nuggets and humor that will help you take responsibility for your own happiness. A *'must read'* book."

GERALD G. JAMPOLSKY, M.D.
Author of *Love Is Letting Go of Fear*

"I love Andrew's work—it is brilliant, insightful, fun and helpful. Enjoy reading and savoring his wisdom."

MARK VICTOR HANSEN
Co-author *Chicken Soup for the Soul*

"FOLLOW YOUR HEART is a smash! It feels like coming home, like being born again with no hang-ups!"

OBADIAH S. HARRIS, Ph.D.
President, The Philosophical Research Society, U.S.A.

"FOLLOW YOUR HEART contains much wisdom. The profound message is presented in a joyful, easy-to-learn-from manner."

BERNIE S. SEIGEL, M.D.
Author of *Love, Medicine and Miracles*

FOLLOW YOUR HEART
written and illustrated by
Andrew Matthews

PRICE STERN SLOAN
a member of Penguin Putnam Inc.
New York

FOLLOW YOUR HEART
Copyright © 1997 by Andrew Matthews
and Seashell Publishers

Published by Price Stern Sloan, Inc.
a member of Penguin Putnam Inc.
375 Hudson Street
New York, NY 10014

Layout and design by Seashell Publishers
Printed in Singapore by C.O.S. Printers Pte Ltd

3 5 7 9 10 8 6 4 2

Library of Congress Cataloguing-in-Publication Data
Matthews, Andrew
Follow Your Heart / written and illustrated by Andrew Matthews.
p. cm.
ISBN 0-8431-7491-9 (alk. paper)
1. Conduct of life.   I. Title.
BF637.C5M35   1999
158-dc21   98-47058
                                                                  CIP

Also by the same author:
"Being Happy!"
"Making Friends"

IN MEMORY

of my father, Peter,
who was living proof that you can
follow your heart and have a ball.

DEDICATED

to my precious wife, Julie.
Thank you for your endless guidance and support,
and for the joy you bring.

THANK YOU

to editors
Vimala Sundram of Capital Communications
Ayesha Harben of Ayesha Harben and Associates
to Celia Painter of The Media Works,

to Sharryn Cremer and Greta Connelly for your efforts
in typesetting and for your day to day help in the office,

to Les Hoffman, thank you for your advice,

and to my sister, Jane Thomas, thank you for your help.

CONTENTS

"The company has decided to recognize your contribution!"

FOLLOW YOUR HEART

The Ten Concepts:

1. We are here to learn lessons, and the world is our teacher.

2. The universe has no favorites.

3. Your life is a perfect reflection of your beliefs.

4. The moment you get too attached to things, people, money ... you screw it up.

5. What you focus on in life expands.

6. Follow your heart!

7. God is never going to come down from a cloud and say, *"You now have permission to be successful!"*

8. When you fight life, life always wins.

9. How do you love people? Just accept them.

10. Our mission in life is not to change the world— our mission is to change ourselves.

I

WE ARE HERE
TO LEARN LESSONS,
AND THE WORLD IS
OUR TEACHER.

When we fail to
learn a lesson,
we get to take it again
… and again!
Once we have learned
the lesson, we move on
to the next one.

(And we never run out of lessons!)

Lesson 1
debt for beginners
Lesson 2
serious debt
lesson 3
poverty I and II
Lesson 4
massive Debt
lesson 5
poverty (phd.)
IOU
ANDREW MATTHEWS

CHAPTER 1

Why Do I Need Disasters?
Lessons
Living and Learning

SOMETHING CAN BE STARING YOU IN THE FACE ...

When I was ten, my most prized possession was my football—I ate with it, slept with it, and I polished it weekly ... instead of my shoes. I knew all about football—but on some other things, like where babies came from, I was a little hazy.

One afternoon I was playing in the street and I lost my precious ball. I looked everywhere. I figured someone had stolen it.

Eventually I spotted a woman who seemed to be hiding it under her jacket. So I marched up and asked her: "What do you think you're doing with my football stuck up your shirt?"

It turned out that she didn't have my football ... but that afternoon I learned where babies come from—and what a woman looks like when she is nine months pregnant.

Later that day, I also found my ball.

What fascinated me most of all was why I had never noticed a pregnant woman before the age of ten ... and why, from then onward, I seemed to be surrounded by them.

IN A NUTSHELL

We reach points in our life when we are ready for new information. Until then, something can be staring us in the face but we don't see it.

WHY DO I NEED DISASTERS?

The only time most of us ever learn anything is when we get hit over the back of the head! Why? Because it's easier not to change. So we keep doing what we're doing until we hit a brick wall. Take our health for example. When do we change diets and start exercising? When our body is falling apart—when the doctor says: "If you don't change your lifestyle, you'll kill yourself!" Suddenly we're motivated!

In relationships—when do we usually tell each other how much we care? When the marriage is falling apart, when the family is falling apart!

In school—when do we finally knuckle down and study? When we're about to fail. In business—when do we try new ideas and make the tough decisions? When we can't pay our bills. When do we finally learn about customer service? After the customers have left!

When do we usually pray? When our life is falling apart! "Dear Lord, I know I haven't spoken to you since the last time the yogurt hit the fan ..."

We learn our biggest lessons when things get rough. When have you made the most important decisions in your life? When you were on your knees—after disasters, after knock-backs, when you've been kicked in the head. That's when we say to ourselves: *"I'm sick of being broke, sick of being kicked around. I'm tired of being mediocre. I'm going to do something."* Success we celebrate—but we don't learn too much. Failure hurts—and that's when we get educated. In retrospect, we usually notice "disasters" were turning points.

Effective people don't go looking for problems, but when they get smacked in the mouth, they ask themselves: *"How do I need to change what I'm thinking and what I'm doing? How can I be better than I am now?"* Losers ignore all the warning signs. When the roof falls in, they ask: *"Why does everything happen to me?"*

We are creatures of habit. We keep doing what we are doing until we are forced to change.

Mary gets dumped by boyfriend Al. Devastated, she locks herself in her bedroom for a week. Then gradually she starts to call old friends and meet new ones. She soon moves house and changes jobs. Within six months she is happier and more confident than she has ever been in her life. She looks back on the "disaster" of losing Al as the best thing that ever happened to her.

Fred gets the sack. Unable to find work, he starts his own little business. For the first time in his life he is his own boss, and doing what he really wants to do. He still has his problems, but his life has new meaning and excitement—and all out of apparent disaster.

SO IS LIFE A SERIES OF PAINFUL DISASTERS?

Not necessarily. The universe is always nudging us with gentle signals. When we ignore the signals, it nudges us with a sledgehammer.

Growth is most painful when we resist it.

ANDREW MATTHEWS

LESSONS

Some things are beyond our understanding ... when a child is born with AIDS, when a young mother is gunned down in a hold up, when a whole village is wiped out by flood, we are left asking: "Why?" For these things there seem to be no answers. But on a different level—on the "everyday life level"—we can find some clues.

Have you ever noticed that certain things happen to certain people? Louise gets fired about every six months, Frank seems to get sued every year, Jim gets food poisoning on vacation.

Certain things *don't* seem to happen to certain people. Jim never gets fired, Louise never goes to court and Frank doesn't send postcards from the hospital.

Particular people get particular lessons. We can react to all of this in one of three ways. We either say:

- "MY LIFE IS A SERIES OF LESSONS I NEED, HAPPENING IN PERFECT ORDER." (The healthiest approach, guarantees maximum peace of mind.)
- "LIFE IS A LOTTERY, BUT I MAKE THE MOST OF WHATEVER COMES ALONG." (The next best option—offers average quality of life.)
- "WHY DO BAD THINGS ALWAYS HAPPEN TO ME?" (Guarantees maximum misery and frustration.)

We are continually being presented with lessons. *Unless we learn the lessons, we get to take them again ... and again ... and again.*

Call it a divine plan, call it the natural unfolding of events, it is happening. Like it or hate it, it is happening. Take responsibility or claim you're a victim, fight it or ignore it, it's happening. It has been happening all your life. Every time your neighbor abused you, each time a salesman ripped you off or a lover walked out on you, there was a lesson staring you in the face.

If we are miserable seven days a week, it's likely we've missed a lesson. When we keep losing jobs, lovers, money ... it's a sign that we haven't been paying attention. As one lady remarked: *"I keep getting the same old problems in a different pair of trousers!"*

The worst thing we can ever say is: *"It's not fair!"*

IN A NUTSHELL

We are not here to be *punished*.
We are here to be e*ducated*. Every
event has the potential to transform us,
and disasters have the greatest potential to
change our thinking. ACT AS IF EVERY EVENT
HAS A PURPOSE, AND YOUR LIFE WILL HAVE PURPOSE.
Figure out why you needed an experience, conquer it, and you won't need
it again.

I COULD DO ANYTHING BUT THAT!

We usually want to postpone our most important lessons. We might look at our rocky relationship with our mother and say: "After all the nasty things she has said, I could do *anything* but love her." Right! You probably *could* do almost anything but that right now. That is why it is your lesson. Growth is about breaking new ground!

MY EX HUSBAND IS A PAIN IN THE BUTT!

Divorcing someone doesn't mean our class with them is over. If the marriage is finished, but we're still blaming them for our misery and our mortgage, we are still hooked to them! We remain linked because there is more to learn.

You say: "But the guy is a turkey! I could do *anything*, but forgive him!" Forgiving him probably *would* be the hardest thing—and it's probably something you are not good at—so you are getting a chance to practice it. You can postpone the class, but if you want your life (and your health) to improve, you'll have to take it sometime. While we believe that someone is ruining our life, that belief will make it true for us. It might seem like *they* are in the way of our happiness. Actually it's us in the way—because we choose how we see people.

MY BOSS IS A CREEP. IT'S NOT MY FAULT—HE NEEDS TO STOP BEING A CREEP! (SO WHAT'S MY LESSON?)

While you remain convinced that your boss is a certified creep, he'll be a creep. And it's OK to think he's a creep. At the point *you* choose to change—e.g. focus on his good points, stop judging him, even empathize a little—the problem will evaporate.

How, you say? There are a thousand possibilities ... a) He may respond to your change of attitude and begin to open up, b) He may be transferred to another department, c) You may get another job, d) He may get another job, e) You may get to like the guy. (Really!) How often do we befriend people who, initially, we couldn't tolerate?

When you change, your situation changes. It is law. You don't have to figure out how it will happen. Your transformation alters your circumstance. But your change must be genuine. You say: "I'll put up with Fred but I still know he's a jerk!" But that isn't a major transformation on your part!

HOW LONG WILL IT TAKE? As long as it takes you to change.

WHY DON'T I JUST LEAVE THIS JOB NOW? You can do that. But chances are you'll find yourself working for another creep— it's all part of the great cosmic curriculum!

MAYBE IF I GO TO A NEW CITY, I CAN MAKE A NEW START

Wrong! *Usually, the best place to make a new start is where you are!* Take Fred, who owes money to half the neighborhood. Fred says to himself: "Maybe I need to move!" But when he moves, he'll take his thoughts and habit patterns with him—and they are what shape his life. Fred changes cities and attracts the same situations, and another bunch of angry creditors.

If you are a spendthrift, and you migrate to Argentina, you'll still be a spendthrift. The best advice to Fred: *"Before changing your address, consider changing your thinking!"*

LESSONS CHASE US AROUND THE WORLD

In Jill's family, money was a dirty word. Her parents weren't especially short of it, but she was embarrassed to ask for it, they didn't want to share it and the whole family argued about it. She left home and went to live in Barcelona ... and married a fellow who makes plenty of money but won't give her any! When you step off the plane, your lessons are there to greet you!

IF ONLY I COULD GO TO TIBET, MAYBE I COULD FIND THE MEANING OF LIFE ...

Some of us get grand ideas about traveling to distant lands to find the meaning of life ... Jim treks off to the Himalayas. One day, while sitting on a dusty street corner, racked with diarrhea and dreaming of a warm bath, he has a blinding flash: "Maybe I can 'do enlightenment' at the Ritz Carlton!"

It sounds romantic finding the meaning of life in Tibet, but enlightenment in Tibet is for Tibetans! The meaning of life for most of us is probably in the suburbs.

LESSONS WE FEAR

The only way to beat fear is to face it. Because we are always attracting the learning experiences we need, we often attract the experiences that we fear.

Therefore, if you are scared witless of being in debt, chances are you'll get to find out all about it. If you fear loneliness, you'll attract that. If you fear embarrassment, you'll fall on your face. It's life's way of encouraging us to grow.

IN A NUTSHELL

We are each a cause. Our thoughts attract and create circumstances. As we change, we attract different circumstances. Until we learn a lesson about debt, or work, or lovers, we either, a) stay stuck on the same lesson, or b) keep getting the same lesson in different packages.

Life goes like this. We get hit by little pebbles—as a kind of warning. When we ignore the pebbles, we get hit by a brick. Ignore the brick and we get wiped out by a boulder. If we're honest, we can see where we have ignored the warning signs. And then we have the nerve to say: "Why me?"

LIVING AND LEARNING

"It's only by going down into the abyss
that we recover the treasures of life.
Where you stumble
there lies your treasure.
The very cave you are afraid to enter
turns out to be the source of
what you were looking for."
Joseph Campbell

L ife doesn't always have to be painful—but pain is still the main reason we change. Until we are in pain, we can pretend. Our ego says: "I'm fine." When things hurt enough, for example, when we are lonely enough, or scared enough, we become vulnerable. Our ego has no more answers, and we open up. Pain encourages us to get serious.

It's always easier to be philosophical about *other people's pain!* We look at Jim and say: "Going broke was a huge learning experience for him." We look at Mary and say: "That divorce helped her to stand on her own feet." We all agree: "Challenges make you stronger."

But when our own challenges come along, we're not so enthusiastic. We say: "Lord, why this? Give me a *convenient* challenge!" Unfortunately, real challenges aren't convenient.

IF ONLY I COULD HAVE SOME QUALITY PEOPLE IN MY LIFE . . .

We might look at our life and say: *"If I didn't have to deal with my lazy husband and these rowdy kids, I could get about my personal growth . . .* " Wrong! They are your personal growth.

20

The people in our life are our teachers. Husbands who snore and leave cupboard doors open, "ungrateful" children, neighbors who park across the driveway ... Only for so long can we tell ourselves: "I'd be happier if these guys got their act together!"

If your wife makes you angry, then your project is to deal with anger effectively. And you have the perfect person to help you do it right in your home. A practice partner! What fortune!

You might say: "I'll divorce her! That will fix it!" But it will fix it only until you marry someone else who makes you just as angry.

IN A NUTSHELL

Every person who walks into your life is a teacher. Even if they drive you nuts, they teach you because they show you where your limits are. Just because people are your teachers doesn't mean you have to like them.

STEP BY STEP

Life is a bit like a ladder. To move up, we have to fix the step we're on—whether it's work, relationships, money, whatever. Once the step is fixed, we move to the next step. People handle their steps in different ways:

"I hate this step—I want to be on a different one." That's when we stay stuck.

"I want someone else's ladder." That's called jealousy.

"To hell with this ladder—I'm jumping off." That is called suicide.

Whenever we are stuck, we might ask ourselves: "What haven't I fixed?"

WHEN DOES LIFE GET SIMPLER?

It doesn't! But you can learn to handle it better. When you sign up for planet Earth, you get the whole "life class," which means *as long as you are breathing, school is in session.*

We keep thinking that once we get past pre-school, grade school, puberty ... once we go to work, life will get easier. It doesn't. No one ever warned us! No wonder we get frustrated.

We look at other people who, from a distance, seem to be on easy street, but they're dealing with their own problems ... Bill appears to be cruising. He retires on a healthy pension—the house is paid off, he drives a nice car, eats in fine restaurants, he takes overseas vacations, plays some golf. What we don't know is that he's suing his insurance company, the roof is leaking, his son is on cocaine, and some burglar will have his video recorder by this time tomorrow.

All of us are constantly challenged.

ANOTHER REASON LIFE DOESN'T GET SIMPLER ...

When things get too easy, we look for more problems. We say to ourselves: "I can do this with my eyes shut! I need a challenge." When life gets too simple, we start a family! When the house is paid off, we buy a bigger one! It's not just the world that complicates our life, we do.

22

SO HOW DO I KEEP FROM GOING CRAZY?

It's how you deal with it.

- Never tell yourself: "I can't relax and enjoy myself until … " Relax and enjoy while you're in the middle of things.
- Continually ask yourself: "What am I learning from this?"

We never get our lives tidied into neat little boxes. People see happiness as some kind of distant mirage—like they are crawling through the desert and there's a sign ahead that says "HAPPINESS," and they say: *"If I can just make it THERE, then I'll be happy."* They have it logically figured out: "We can't be happy now because we're having the bathroom remodeled. But next month … " And next month the kids have the flu, the cat's in heat, the in-laws are coming to stay, and they say: "Around next April … "

TEACHING OTHERS A LESSON

Have you ever been very excited about a book you just read? You take it to a friend and say: "Read this, it's fantastic!" Then you hold your breath, waiting for their enthusiastic phone call. But they never call!

MATTHEWS

Six months later you ask for your book to find, a) they never read it, and b) they've lost it. The lesson here—which applies to "friendly advice" as well as books—is, that just because you're ready for information doesn't mean everyone else is ready.

IN A NUTSHELL

If people aren't asking you, they usually don't want the information!

SO WHAT AM I TO LEARN FROM THIS?

Reflect on your life to this point, and you'll perhaps see a reason why you took the path you did. You will see people dotted through your past—teachers, lovers and even strangers on airplanes—who gave you direction. You'll remember a book you found in a junk shop that shaped your thinking. You will recall "accidents"—heartaches, illnesses, failures and financial crises that made you stronger or taught you compassion. You'll see "disasters" that in retrospect were more likely part of a larger scheme. You might get that feeling that you have been learning a series of lessons, in just the right order. You might sense that one thing was always leading to another.

In the beginning, it's difficult to see disasters in perspective. There's a lag time, while we're telling ourselves: "This is not part of the approved script—sorry God, you made a big mistake!" It takes us six months to figure how getting fired was actually part of a plan!

The universe is a patient and persistent teacher. Watch the signals and life runs relatively smoothly. But fall asleep at the wheel and "Whammo!"—you attract a major learning experience—a bankruptcy, a divorce, a heart attack.

Fred might argue: "There's no life path. Everyone has to be somewhere at sometime." As he expands his awareness, he might notice his own unfolding curriculum.

SO WHERE ARE MY NEXT LESSONS?

They are usually right under our nose—and often we know exactly what they are, and we're hoping they'll go away!

II

THE UNIVERSE
HAS NO
FAVORITES.

**Your success and happiness
depend on natural
laws and principles—
and how you use them.**

CHAPTER 2

The Law of the Seed
Cause and Effect
As You Get Better, the Game Gets Bigger
Discipline
Be Adaptable!

UNIVERSAL LAWS

When the great spiritual teachers told their stories, they spoke of sowing seeds and fetching water. Of course, they talked of seasons, and crops and fish because the people of the time understood farming and fishing. But it goes deeper than that. Nature's laws are all there is.

Whether you are a goat herder or computer programmer, the same rules apply.

ANDREW MATTHEWS

THE LAW OF THE SEED

In my first book, "BEING HAPPY!", I talk about some of nature's laws. This chapter expands on those principles. We begin with the law of the seed ...

The lesson of the seed is: *"You reap your harvest after you do the work."* You dig the soil and water the seed (effort), wait a while (patience) and then you pick your beans. Effort + patience = results.

This principle is often lost on people. They say: *"If I plant beans today, what will I get back tomorrow?"* And the answer is: *"Wet bean seeds."* The law of the seed says: *"You plant today, and you harvest ... LATER!"* Plant beans now; pick beans in four months. When everybody grew their own food, people probably understood this concept better. But this is the age of instant noodles.

Fred says: *"If I had a decent job, then I would really work hard. But all I do is wash dishes, so to heck with it."* Wrong, Fred! If you become the best dish washer in town, someone will notice you, or someone will promote you, or you'll feel so good about yourself that you'll one day go and do something you really want to do.

Effort first, harvest second. It's a principle. You can't reverse the process. Mary says: *"Promote me, and then I'll quit sleeping on the job."* Frank says: *"Pay me more and I'll stop being sick."* Jane says: *"If I had a good marriage, I'd be nice to my husband."*

Credit cards and mail order catalogues encourage us to buy now, pay no interest until February and go broke in March. It's playing with the same principles. Earn now, pay later works better than buy now, pay later.

Another lesson we learn in the garden: when you plant a dozen bean seeds, you don't get a dozen bean plants. Fred plants his bean seeds. Some get burned up. Some get blown away. The bugs get a few. The birds take three or four. Fred is left with two little bean plants, and he says: "It's not fair!" It's life.

To find even a few good friends, you begin with a lot of acquaintances. To find the ideal employee, you interview fifty. To find a few regular customers, you begin with a hundred. To find the perfect spaghetti marinara, you eat in a lot of restaurants.

Many of your ideas, employees, and even your friends will get blown away or taken by the birds. This is not something you fight, it's something you understand. It is something you prepare for.

CAUSE AND EFFECT

If your life is stagnant, you need to look at what you are putting in. You never hear anyone saying: *"I rise at dawn, I'm exercising my body, I'm studying, I'm nurturing my relationships, I'm putting maximum effort into my work—and NOTHING GOOD is happening in my life."* Your life is an energy system. If nothing good is happening in your life, it's your fault. Once you acknowledge that your input shapes your circumstances, you cease to be a victim.

We might look at other people's lives and say: *"What happened to the law of cause and effect?"* Ralph gets a promotion and we ask: *"How did he deserve that?"* The neighbors celebrate forty years of happy marriage, and we say: *"Why are they so lucky?"* It can be confusing, but the same rules of cause and effect operate for everyone.

We get in life what we ask for. Bruce charms his women with diamonds and perfume. When they walk out on him, he claims he's been used for his money. If you go fishing with diamonds for bait, you'll catch fish that like diamonds! Is that a surprise?

Wendy hits the town in plunging necklines. Meanwhile, she's angry that men only want her for her body. The guys spot the cleavage a block away! Where's the mystery?

IN A NUTSHELL

If we are honest with ourselves, we can list almost everything that's ever happened to us—and see how we helped create it. Don't worry about whether the laws of the universe are delivering for your neighbor. Watch the law of cause and effect at work in your own life—in your own relationships, your own successes and your own disappointments. You will have greater peace of mind.

AS YOU GET BETTER, THE GAME GETS BIGGER

When we succeed at a little game, we get to play in a bigger game ... and a bigger game.

When we start school, we begin in grade one. Next we move up to grade two, three and so on. It's an effective system, and the principle is, *"When you get BETTER, the game gets BIGGER."*

Somewhere along the way, people lose track of this concept. Frank is struggling to make his car payments. In twenty years of working, he has saved exactly eighty-seven cents. He says: *"If I had a million bucks, I'd know how to take care of it!"* Wrong! Your current mission, Frank, is to learn to save ten dollars. Hundreds come before thousands ... and you work your way up to the million.

Candy is a singer in a local bar and she wants to be a star. She says: *"If I had an audience of a thousand, I'd really give them a show. But if you think I'm going to waste my talents on six losers, you're crazy!"* When Candy learns how to put on a show for six, she'll get twelve, and then a hundred, and one day she'll pack a thousand.

Jim sells insurance from a little office. He has one employee, and he's about to sack her! Jim says: *"If I only had a dozen good staff ..."* No Jim, it will never work with a team of twelve until you can make it work with a team of two.

Life is a gradual progression. The question is always: "WHAT ARE YOU DOING WITH WHAT YOU HAVE?" While the answer is "not much," nothing gets better.

IN A NUTSHELL

The universe rewards effort, not excuses.

ONE THING LEADS TO ANOTHER

When my world seemed dull, I used to look at people who led fascinating lives and wonder: *"How did their life become so sweet?"* I discovered that they made a start, somewhere. That small start led to something else and to something else.

Sometimes we can make the mistake of being too selective. We might reject a job offer, reasoning: *"It's not quite the job I want."* If it's all you've got for the moment, grab it, master it, and watch it lead you from one thing to another. If you have nothing big going for you, start small. Jump in the water.

Entrepreneur John McCormack tells the story of how his friend, Nick, got his first job in America. Nick was an immigrant. He had no money and spoke no English, and he applied for a dishwashing job in an Italian restaurant. Before his interview with the boss, Nick went into the restaurant's bathroom and scrubbed it clean. He then took a toothbrush and cleaned between every tile until the bathroom was completely spotless. By the time Nick had his interview, the boss was trying to figure out: "What's happened to the toilets?" It was Nick's way of saying: "I'm serious about washing dishes."

Nick got the job. A week later, the salad maker quit and Nick was on his way to becoming a chef. I think of Nick and his toothbrush when people tell me: "There are no jobs out there!"

IN A NUTSHELL

Start anywhere you can. Give your best shot to whatever is in front of you, and opportunity will begin to find you. It's called developing a reputation. It's called *"one thing leads to another."*

THE FROG PRINCIPLE

There is an often quoted story of a frog and a bucket of water. It illustrates the law of deterioration ...

If you take an intelligent, happy frog and drop him into a bucket of boiling water, what will the frog do? Jump out! Instantly, the frog decides: "This is no fun—I'm gone!"

If you take the same frog, or a relative, and drop him into a bucket of cold water, put the bucket on the stove and gradually heat up the bucket, what then? The frog's relaxing ... a few minutes later he says to himself: "It seems warm in here." Soon enough, you have a cooked frog.

The moral of the story? Life happens gradually. Like the frog, we can be fooled, and suddenly it's too late. We need to be aware of what is happening.

QUESTION—If you woke tomorrow forty pounds heavier, would you be worried? Sure you would! You'd be calling the hospital: "Emergency! I'm fat!" But when things happen gradually, a pound this month, a pound next month, we tend to let it go.

32

When you overspend on your budget by ten dollars in one day, it's no big deal. But if you do it again tomorrow, and the next day, and the next, you end up broke. For people who go broke, put on weight, get divorced, it usually isn't one big disaster—it's a bit today and a bit tomorrow—and then one day "kaboom!"—and they say: "What happened?"

Life is accumulative. One thing ADDS to another—like the drops of water that wear away the rock. The frog principle is telling us to watch the trends. Each day, we ask ourselves: "Where am I heading? Am I fitter, healthier, happier, more prosperous than I was last year?" If not, we need to change what we are doing.

Here's the scary thing—there's no standing still. You're either gaining or slipping.

DISCIPLINE

Have the discipline to do little things you don't like, and you can spend your life doing the big things you do like.

Discipline is not everyone's favorite word. In popularity, it probably slots somewhere between *dentist* and *diarrhea*. But self discipline makes all the difference. Life is a trade off between instant pleasure and long term reward.

Self discipline in the little things—*studying instead of TV*—leads to a big thing—*better qualifications*. Self discipline in the little things—*three sessions a week at the gym*—leads to a big thing—a *healthier life*.

Self discipline in the little things—*saving twenty dollars a day instead of blowing it on booze*—leads to a big thing—*your own apartment.*

The key to self discipline is not an iron will. It is knowing WHY you want something. If you really know why you want to get out of debt, it's easier to save. If you're clear about why you want to improve your qualifications, it's easier to study.

Something else about discipline: when you are self disciplined, you don't need to get discipline from anywhere else. As a result, you run your own life and people don't tell you what to do.

When you don't have self discipline, you get it from outside. People who can't discipline themselves often slot into jobs where they take orders. People who have absolutely no self discipline get themselves locked up!

ORDER

The first law of expansion is "order." For something to grow, it needs system.

Look at a flower, cut an orange, check out the symmetry of a tree or a beehive. There is discipline. Nature keeps what is essential and gets rid of the garbage. It's called organization.

If you want your business to grow, you must have method. If you want your life to blossom, you need some order in it.

Fred says: *"My office is a mess, but it's an organized mess. I'm actually very efficient!"* Oh really? I can just imagine Fred being wheeled into an operating theater for brain surgery, to find the medical team standing amongst piles of needles, bandages and old bottles. The surgeon says: "Relax Fred. It's a mess in here but we're in total control!"

Wherever performance counts, there is organization. Firemen always know where to find their helmets, ambulance drivers have one spot for car keys!

Nothing blooms out of a mess. Organize your filing cabinet. Clean up your garage.

Something else you'll notice. "As within, so without"—your environment reflects your thinking. Usually, when your house is a mess, so is your life.

NO EFFORT IS WASTED

Take a block of ice that's been frozen to minus twenty degrees fahrenheit, and start heating it. For some time, nothing happens. Lots of energy for no visible result. Suddenly, at thirty-two degrees, it melts. Water!

Keep heating. Again, lots of energy and no excitement. Then, at around two hundred and twelve degrees fahrenheit, bubbles and steam! It boils!

The principle? It's possible to put lots of energy into something—e.g. a block of ice, a project, a career—yet it seems like nothing is happening. Actually, your energy is already producing change, but you just can't see it. Continue to put the energy in and you will surely see a transformation. Remember the principle, and you don't panic so much—and you don't despair.

I like to picture my life as a pinball game. Every time I make any effort—tidy my desk, write a book, help a friend, practice drawing, pay a bill, try and fail—I'm scoring points. I think of all my efforts as adding to my "universal credit". I never know how many points I'll need for my next reward. It helps me enjoy what I'm doing rather than demand instant results. And every so often, usually when I least expect it, bingo—a new opportunity, an invitation, a check in the mail.

WAVES

Life happens in waves. We know about sound waves, light waves, brain waves, microwaves. In non scientific terms waves demonstrate that *things have a tendency to travel in bunches.*

This means family crises, wedding invitations and car repairs also tend to travel in bunches. Bearing this in mind is helpful. When you strike a month without bills, you say to yourself: *"I'll put something aside for the next wave."* When you get swamped by the next wave, you say to yourself: *"I know about these waves—this is only temporary."*

BE ADAPTABLE!

We live in a world where things are always changing. The seasons come and go, the tide comes in and out, inflation goes up and down, people get hired and fired ... You would think we would learn that the underlying law of the universe is change! Instead we get angry.

In high school biology, we study the law of *natural selection*—adapting to change. We learn, for example, that if you are a green bug in a brown field, and you don't change the color of your skin, you are in big trouble. You can argue: "The field should be gree it used to be green ..." But very soon, no more bug. The law is brutal—"ADAPT or DISAPPEAR!" It's a shame more biology teachers never said: "TAKE NOTE—THIS IS A LESSON OF LIFE—BE ADAPTABLE."

In the corporate world, things change, and even the experts can get it wrong.

In 1927, Harry Warner of Warner Brothers Pictures said: *"Who the hell wants to hear actors talk?"*

In 1943, Thomas Watson, chairman of IBM, said: *"I think there is a world market for about five computers."*

In 1977, Ken Olsen, president of Digital Equipment Corporation, said: *"There is no reason for any individual to have a computer in their home."*

What is true today may not be true tomorrow. What works today may not work tomorrow. The only constant we have is change. If you leave home for three months, you'll find your kids have changed. Suddenly your baby is calling you "Daddy!" It's not a question of fair or unfair. Everything is moving.

IN A NUTSHELL

Happy people don't just accept change, they *embrace* it. They are the people who say: *"Why would I want my next five years to be like my last five?"*

III

YOUR LIFE IS A PERFECT REFLECTION OF YOUR BELIEFS.

When you change your deepest beliefs about the world, your life changes accordingly.

CHAPTER 3

Beliefs
My Job Is the Problem!
Making Money
Spoil Yourself!
It's Not What Happens to You . . .

BELIEFS

"The thing always happens that you believe in; and the belief in a thing makes it happen."
Frank Lloyd Wright

When people argue for their limitations they say: "I can't do 'X' because . . . " The common excuse is: *"It's just the way I AM."* More likely the truth is: *"It's just the way I THINK I AM."* We can learn about our beliefs by studying fish. (The following experiment was conducted at the Woods Hole Oceanographic Institute).

Get yourself an aquarium. Divide it in half with a clear glass wall, so now you have a kind of fish "duplex." Now find yourself a barracuda—we'll call him Barry—and a mullet. (Barracuda eat mullet). Put one fish on each side. In a flash, Barry will head for the mullet and . . . thump . . . hit the glass wall at full throttle. He'll turn around and come back for another shot . . . thump!

Over a period of weeks, Barry will get a very sore nose. Eventually he'll figure that mullet hunting equals pain, and quit chasing the mullet. You can then remove the glass wall, and guess what! He will stay on his side of the tank for the rest of his life. Barry will happily starve to death, with the mullet swimming just inches away. He knows his limits, and he won't step outside them.

Is Barry's a pitiful tale? It is actually the story of every human being. We don't run into glass plates—we run into teachers, parents and friends

"You say that I always think I'm right—
but that's where you're wrong!"

who tell us where we fit and what we can do. Worst of all, we run into our own beliefs. Our beliefs define our territory, we argue for it and we won't step outside it.

Barry the Barracuda says: "I gave it my best shot once—so now I just swim in circles." We say: "I gave my studies/ my marriage/ my job my best shot once before ... "

We create our own glass cage, and we think it is reality. Actually, it's just what we believe. And how attached are people to their beliefs? Just try talking religion or politics at a dinner party!

BUT I *KNOW* I'M RIGHT!

Isn't it funny? We all believe something slightly different about the world—and we all *know* that what we believe is right.

Why? Because we *are* right! Fred believes that life is tough and that he has to work seventy hours a week to survive. Looking through the employment section in the newspaper, he sees a position advertised in the next suburb ... *"flexible hours, exciting travel opportunities, company car, top salary."* Fred says: "Too good to be true—there must be a catch!" Fred keeps looking. He spots another ad, and this time the job is a two hour drive across town. *No car, long hours, low pay.* Fred says: "This is worth a closer look!"

He attends an interview. The boss says: "Our products are revolting, our customers hate us, the owner is a crook. If you want to work here you're crazy!" And Fred says: "When can I start?"

Fred proves that his theory about life is correct—he is miserable, but at least he is happy that he is miserable.

While growing up, teachers, parents and friends tell us things like: "You're hopeless at mathematics, you sing like a duck and you can't draw to save yourself." They say: "Life is tough, you'll always be broke, blame the government ... *That's your script. Go live it!*" And we go and act it out, almost like we're in a play. We believe it, even if it ruins our life.

Suggest to Fred that he might want to "unbelieve" something he has accepted for forty years and he will probably get very upset: "I've been miserable for forty years with this belief system. You want me to give it up now, and admit I helped create this mess?"

Most of us would rather be right than happy.

WHAT'S MY STORY?

Most of us have a "story." We label ourselves ... "I'm a school teacher," "I'm a grandmother," "I'm a new age guy." Our "story" is like a software program, lodged between our ears and controlling our life. It's our personal marketing package. We take it to work, we take it on vacation. At parties we drag it out ... "I'm a divorcee." "I was an abused child." "I'm on the spiritual path!" We spend our lives trying to fit the story. We buy our cars and clothes, and choose our friends to fit the story.

Jim is a doctor. He tells himself: "I have to act like doctors act and talk like doctors talk. I need a house in a doctor's kind of street and I need a doctor's kind of hobby." He has his role all figured out, but poor Jim is as dull as a dog biscuit.

Trying to fit a "story" makes us miserable. If my story is "I'm a school teacher," when I lose my job, I don't know what I am. If my story is "I'm the perfect hostess," I set myself up for misery because no evening is perfect. When the neighbors come for dinner, and I burn the carrots, I'm devastated.

Here's the crunch ... YOU ARE NOT YOUR STORY AND NOBODY CARES ANYWAY. You don't belong in a category or a box.

You are a human being having a *series of experiences*. When you quit dragging a story around, you never have to "look the part."

As I write this, I'm thinking of my Swedish friends, Anna and Per-Erik. Somewhere in their late seventies or early eighties, they still travel the world. Per-Erik rollerblades on his grandson's skates and surfs the Internet. Anna loves to dance until four in the morning. They don't seem to have "a story"—they have spirit.

Do you recognize the following *stories?*

"I'M A VERY IMPORTANT PERSON—PEOPLE SHOULD TREAT ME ACCORDINGLY!" Some people insist that everyone else should recognize them, know how rich they are and how many degrees they've got. While you demand that other people think you're important, you suffer because your happiness is in their hands. Forget about "being important"—it's too stressful. The minute you don't have to "be important", you can relax. The less you demand appreciation from others, the more you get.

"I'M THE SORT OF PERSON WHO NEVER ... (travels first class, goes skinny dipping, goes to the theater, wears dinner suits, eats sashimi)." When we tell ourselves "I never" or "I always" it keeps us in the box, but it's only our *story* talking. We have other stories, like "I'm very sensitive—things upset me." "I'm a real man." "I'm a Sagittarian so I always ... "

"I'M TOO OLD TO ... " My mother started to write her first book when she was sixty-seven. She died at sixty-eight, and never finished the book. But she made a start, and was happier for it. There's only one way to go, and that is to be learning, and loving what you do, right up to the last minute. If you have a book half written, or a house or a business half built, and you get hit by a bus, are you going to worry?

IN A NUTSHELL

Ask yourself: "What would I do if I had no *story?"*

MATTHEWS

42

SO WHICH OF MY BELIEFS SHOULD I REJECT?

Any beliefs that keep you poor and miserable! If your beliefs don't help you, scrap them! It's not to say they are wrong—they just cause you pain. For a start, beware of beliefs with "should" in them:

People SHOULD return favors!
People SHOULD praise me! If I do a good job, my husband ought to notice.
People SHOULD love me back!
People SHOULD be more considerate!
People SHOULD be grateful!

This *"should list"* might seem a reasonable set of expectations. But what if you didn't hold any of these beliefs? What if people didn't have to agree with you, return favors, notice your good work, love you back? How would that affect your life? You wouldn't get any less respect or appreciation. But when people didn't do these things, you would still be happy.

"Should" beliefs don't help us because reality doesn't understand "should." Things are the way they are. When you criticize reality, reality wins.

YOUR BELIEFS DETERMINE YOUR QUALITY OF LIFE

For example: Let's say you believe that fathers should praise their children and give them lots of presents. Whenever yours doesn't do it, you are upset. So you want to *change Fathers*. Most people never consider the alternative solution: *change beliefs.*

You say: *"But doesn't everyone believe these things?"*

No! Some people don't, and they are happier because of it. Some people don't *expect* others to behave in any particular fashion. As a result, they have more peace of mind.

To see things differently, you don't need willpower, self confidence, or brain surgery. You just need the courage to think the unfamiliar. Next time you are upset, remember it's not so much people who make you angry as your beliefs. Whatever thoughts are causing you pain, they are only thoughts. You can change a thought.

MY JOB IS THE PROBLEM!

When we blame our job, it's usually we who are the problem. Let's say your work is a drag, and you have a matching belief that says *"work is a drag."* If you apply for a job that could be enjoyable, what will happen? Either, a) you won't get the job because they'll see that you are no fun, or b) you'll get the job and you'll manage to make it boring.

Let's say you believe the opposite, that *"work is fun."* If you are in a dead-end-dull job, there will be a point at which you will say: "This is degrading to my spirit and contrary to everything I believe in. I cannot stay here another day." Your most basic beliefs will drive you to find something better, however you do it.

It's not the job, it's what you *believe* that makes the difference.

MAKING MONEY

BUT I DON'T MAKE ENOUGH MONEY!

Mary says: "You don't understand. *It's not my belief system. It's my job.* I don't make enough at my job." Well Mary, why are you working there?

Mary says: "It's all I can do!" (Fine Mary, if that's what you *believe*). Change what you *believe*, and you'll get a new job or start a part time business, rearrange your finances, develop more skills, work for a promotion.

Mary says: "But times are bad. It says so in the newspaper." That's what you *believe*, Mary. What would happen if you didn't believe the newspaper?

Prosperity involves you running your own mind—regardless of what your neighbors and the papers say.

BUT I'M ON A FIXED SALARY . . .

Whether or not you are on a salary, your beliefs determine your prosperity. Take eight people in the same company, on the same wage. We would find some with assets and living well, and some who need a bank

loan to buy a sandwich. The difference—not the money they make but what they believe about money.

If I haven't got the money I want, or if I'm losing it, there's a reason for it—and it's not in the outside world, it is in my inside world.

Lottery winners are a stunning illustration of how belief systems control prosperity. People think money will fix their problems. Yet most people who win lotteries are deeper in debt two years after their windfall than they were before they got the check. Why? Because a belief system that says, "I'm always broke," will soon erase a million dollars.

Recently in Brisbane, Australia, I flicked on the TV to see that a fellow had just won his second lottery. In the interview he said: "The 1.3 million will be very handy because I'm living on welfare at the moment ... " And the guy won a lottery two years ago!

Your bank balance will always match your belief system. When your self image doesn't fit your bank balance, it's easier to change your bank balance. Again, it's our thoughts that control our life, not externals.

THE ADVANTAGES OF BEING BROKE

People who wonder why they are broke never ask the obvious question: "What do I like about being broke?" There are advantages to being broke. For example:
- "I can feel holy ... God will love me—blessed are the poor."
- "I can stay one of the gang. If I remain poor, I won't feel guilty around my friends."
- "I'll get sympathy."
- "I don't have to discipline myself."
- "I don't have to change any habits."
- And best of all ... "I can *blame* other people—and the government!"

If we are honest, we might concede that being broke suits us. Not many people admit to choosing poverty, but it's quite a persuasive list isn't it? Everything we do has a payoff, including "doing poverty."

OUR PARENTS' MONEY BELIEFS

Did your parents often say things like:
- "Money is easy to make."
- "We always have more than enough."
- "Whenever we spend it, more comes."
  Or did they usually say things like:
- "Money is the root of all evil."
- "We can't afford it."
- "Money doesn't grow on trees."

If you are better acquainted with the second list, your parents' belief system probably became your reality. Their struggle became your struggle.

GET COMFORTABLE WITH MONEY!

"Most people are more embarrassed about money than sex."

Have you ever noticed how hard it is to give some people money. They go crazy! "No, it's OK, really. I don't need it." You know they are living on bread and water! They change personality! They get embarrassed. They get insulted! "*I* don't need your money—I'm fine."

Some of us have trouble even talking about money! We lend a friend a week's wages and when we need it back, we don't know how to ask for it: "Ah, you know that … do you remember … well … this isn't really important, and I don't really need it … and it doesn't matter if … how can I put this … I was just wondering about the … " Instead of asking in a sensible manner: "Can you return my money?"

If you are uneasy in a job, or uneasy in a relationship, sooner or later you will part company. If you are uneasy with money—if you are nervous about even talking about it, if money doesn't sit well with you—you will also part company. It's not so much a conscious thing, its a subconscious thing. Things we are awkward with, we avoid.

IN A NUTSHELL

In order to have something in your life, and keep it, you have to be comfortable with it.

TO MAKE MONEY— AND KEEP IT, YOU MUST BE COMFORTABLE WITH MONEY!

IF I HAVE PLENTY, OTHERS WILL GO WITHOUT

This is the silliest belief of all. How many of us grew up believing: "If I'm prosperous, other people will suffer." You know who spreads that idea? The people who don't have it!

If Santa Claus strolled into your living room and dropped a million dollars cash on your coffee table, would it stay there? No! Unless you stuff it under your pillow, you can bet the car dealer will see some of it, your travel agent will see some of it, together with the local restaurants, florists, boutiques and probably the tax man—everyone around you will benefit. Yet many of us grow up believing it's not OK to be prosperous because it will deprive other people. That is nuts!

If you get prosperous, it doesn't have to hurt other people. It can help them.

SPOIL YOURSELF!

"It's a funny thing, life. If you refuse to accept anything but the best, you very often get it."
W. Somerset Maugham

For the world to treat you well, you have to treat yourself well. How can you feel like a mover and shaker when you have holes in your underwear? Fred says: "It doesn't matter if I have holes in my shorts because no one can see them." But here's the crunch, Fred. You know it and your body can feel it. You are the only one that can make you feel special. If you have no pride, nobody can give it to you.

Our home affects the way we feel. Create a space that will uplift you when you walk in the front door. Give your home your personality. Do a deal with your landlord—get him to supply materials and you paint the apartment.

Neatness costs nothing. Better to live in a one room apartment that is *clean* than in a mansion that's a mess. A lady asked my wife, Julie: "What can I do with a decorating budget of twenty dollars?" Julie said: "Buy a broom!"

ENJOY WHAT YOU HAVE

How many of us display our apples and bananas in scratchy old plastic bowls, while our beautiful dishes remain locked in the cupboard? Then we die and leave all the crystal to our kids, so they can smash it! I say, if you have something beautiful, smash it yourself!

I know a fellow who wanted to preserve the resale value of his brand new Volvo, so he had a set of seat covers made out of old bed sheets. Very practical, except you feel like you're riding in a laundry basket!

I learn a lot from Julie about this. Her philosophy is: "Pamper yourself, nourish your body, keep a clean home and you'll feel blessed by life." To quote her: *"Everything affects everything else. The way you walk affects the way you talk. The way you dress affects the way you feel. The care you give to yourself, you will also give to others."* She's the only person I know with shoulder pads in her pajamas! And they are silk pajamas.

Spoil yourself a little. You say: "What does nurturing myself have to do with achieving my goals in life?" Everything! If we feel prosperous, we attract prosperity.

Fred says: "When I get successful, I'll quit living like a rat!"

Wrong! To be a success you have to begin to live it, you have to feel it now.

IN A NUTSHELL

Prosperity is not necessarily a money thing. It is a lifestyle thing.

IT'S NOT WHAT HAPPENS TO YOU, IT'S HOW YOU SEE IT

Accchording to legend, the "alchemists" of the Middle Ages were the people who turned lead into gold—nice work if you can get it! In one sense, we all need to be alchemists: to see beyond surface appearances. Our daily challenge is to take situations that seem unfortunate—missed planes, car accidents, divorces, rude waiters—and transform those situations into lucky breaks.

Does this mean you should pray for a broken leg? No, but if you get one, find some opportunity within the "disaster."

You ask: "What good does this do me?"

It helps on several levels:

- You are more thankful for what life deals you
- You are more peaceful
- You are now riding on the bus of life instead of trying to push it!

The cynic says: "That is being naive. I don't want to be a Pollyanna."

Wrong. As you cease to react in horror to the unexpected, you become more balanced and you move into a position of power.

AS LONG AS YOU BELIEVE SOMETHING IN YOUR LIFE IS A DISASTER, IT WILL UNFOLD AS A CONTINUING DISASTER.

Let's say you are recently divorced and you figure your life is in ruins. As long as you believe that, it will be so. Let's say you get fired at fifty and decide your best years are over. As long as you believe that, it will be so.

Am I saying that while your attitude is negative, you will do nothing to improve your life? Partly, but there's *more* to it. As long as you see only disaster, you willl attract more disaster. Lovers will let you down, bosses will hassle you, accidents will find you, landlords will evict you and it will be a downward spiral. EVENTS WILL UNFOLD ACCORDING TO YOUR EXPECTATIONS.

The minute you change your *beliefs* about the situation, your different thoughts will attract *different people and new opportunities.*

IN A NUTSHELL

EVERY "DISASTER" IN YOUR LIFE IS NOT SO MUCH A DISASTER, AS A SITUATION WAITING FOR YOU TO CHANGE YOUR MIND ABOUT IT. You say: "But does this apply to MY illness, MY bills and MY drunken husband?" You bet it does.

LIFE SHOULDN'T BE THIS MUCH FUN!

I had a woman say to me: "I've never done anything I wanted to all my life." It was as if she was saying: "I've sacrificed - I'm a martyr." I thought: "How sad!"

Life is supposed to be fun! Birds wake up singing every day. Babies laugh for no reason at all. Watch dolphins. Watch dogs in the surf. Who said life is no fun? This is a playful universe. If you inherited the idea that life isn't meant to be fun, understand what that means. It's just a *belief* that you can *"unbelieve."*

Take time out to do things just because they're fun. Working yourself to the bone confirms the idea that "life is a struggle." Be patient with yourself. Even enjoying life takes practice. When life is sweet, and that little voice says: *"It can't last!"* Tell yourself: *"Maybe it's about to get better!"*

IV

**THE MOMENT YOU
GET TOO ATTACHED
TO THINGS,
PEOPLE, MONEY ...
YOU SCREW IT UP!**

**The challenge of life
is to appreciate everything
and attach yourself
to nothing.**

CHAPTER 4

Attachment
Attachment to Money
Giving
Attachment to Lovers

ATTACHMENT

" ... There's such a thing as trying too hard ...
You've got to sing like you don't need the money—
Love like you'll never get hurt—
You've gotta dance like nobody's watching—
It's gotta come from the heart if you want it to work."[1]

When you chase things, they run away. This is true for animals, lovers ... even money! Have you ever met someone cute at a party and they tell you "I'll call you next week!" So you don't go anywhere for a week—not even to the bathroom! You sit by the phone ... and wait. Who calls? Everyone but them!

Did you ever need to sell something, desperately? A car, a house. Who wanted it? Nobody. So you dropped the price. Who cared? Nobody! The principle? *When you're desperate, zilch!*

Talk to any salesperson, whether they're in Lear jets or laundry detergent, and they will tell you the same story. Desperation pulls you into a descending spiral—and the more you worry, the less people buy! What happens when you are in a restaurant and in a hurry for your meal? They lose your order.

I learn about the law of attachment in airports. I have made dozens of author tours in different parts of the world. These trips are usually excursions from six weeks to four months. Until recently, my wife, Julie, ran her own business, and so I mostly went alone.

I found that I could catch a hundred flights, and ninety-nine would be roughly on time. But the one flight home, when I was so desperate to see her and counting the minutes, was always four hours late!

At the end of my last North American book tour, we decided to meet in San Francisco. Julie arrived in San Francisco from Australia while I was still in Portland. I was so used to these delayed departures that I went up to the baggage counter and asked: "How late is the six o'clock to San Francisco?" And the fellow said: "It's not late!"

"Not late?" I was ecstatic. I was about to leap across the counter and hug him when he said: "Do you want to know why it's not late? . . . We've canceled it!" At 10:30 p.m. I got a seat on a plane to San Jose, caught a bus to San Francisco and arrived at Julie's hotel at four in the morning—seven hours late!

Whenever we are desperately involved—emotionally attached to a transaction or a happening—we obstruct it. The flip-side to the principle? Relax a little and *bingo!*

You spend a year and a half without a girl-friend, or boyfriend, and you're desperate. Not even a sniff! Then you give up. You tell yourself: "I don't have to have a partner. I can be happy, single." And suddenly it's feast or famine—they're coming over the walls and out from under the bed!"

An argument is the classic example. What happens when you want someone to change their mind? Will they change it? Not on your life. But stop pushing them and often they come round to your way of thinking.

MATTHEWS

Whenever you are desperate for anything—for someone to call, for your husband to quit smoking, for a promotion, for your boss to show you some appreciation—you create an energy around you that pushes it away.

DETACHMENT versus DISINTEREST

Detachment is not disinterest. It is possible to be detached and still be very determined. People who are detached *and* determined know that *effort and excellence are ultimately rewarded.* They say: *"If I don't win this time, I'll win the next time, or the time after that."*

Let's say you apply for a new job at Haywire Hardware. You are excited about the job and you prepare carefully. You write out your interview speech and you practice it in front of the bathroom mirror. You even get new shoes and a haircut. You arrive early for the interview and you give it your best shot.

What next? You go home and you get on with your life. You enroll in extra study. You plan your next job application. If you get hired by Haywire, you're happy. If not, you are still moving forward.

Disinterested people say: *"Who cares and why bother?"* Desperate people say: *"If I don't get this I'll die!"* When you are determined and detached, you say: *"One way or another, I will get a good job—and I don't care how long it takes."*

ATTACHMENT TO MONEY

"The only people who think more about money than the rich are the poor."
Oscar Wilde

Attachment, which the Buddhists call "grasping," explains why many people struggle to make money. Because money is both a means of survival *and* a symbol of success, most of us are very attached to it—even those of us who insist it doesn't matter. Unfortunately, our desperation for it screws up the whole thing.

Put another way, the more emotional you are about things, the less control you have. Most people are very emotional about money—so they are out of control.

Detachment is a major reason why rich people get richer. They don't care so much—they're not desperate. If you don't have money, you've got to be relaxed enough to know you're going to get it. When you do have it, you need to be comfortable enough with it to keep some of it—and know there's more coming. Also, there's a big difference between a poor person's attitude—*wishing* you had it—and a wealthy person's approach—*believing* you'll get it.

HOW DO I AVOID BEING DESPERATE WHEN I'M DESPERATE?

What do you do specifically? It's attitude.

Never get into the trap of saying: *"I need 'X' to be happy."*

In general, if you are selling your computer, waiting on a phone call, hoping for a promotion, trying to sink a golf putt, waiting for a check in the mail, looking for a husband, relax! You do *everything you can* to make it work, and then you tell yourself: "I don't *need* this to be happy." Forget it and move on, and more often than not, the results will come.

IN A NUTSHELL

On the mental and the physical level, we are dealing with natural laws. Nature doesn't understand desperation! Nature seeks balance, and you can't be desperate *and* balanced. Life doesn't have to be an endless struggle. Let things flow. This is not indifference; it's not forcing things.

You can say: "I don't understand how it all works!" You don't have to understand gravity either. Our challenge is to work with principles—we don't have to understand them.

GIVING

*I*f you want something, give it away! Does that sound crazy? You get more of what you want, by giving away some of what you have. When a farmer wants more seeds, he takes his seeds and gives them to the earth. When you want a smile, you give yours. When you want affection, you give affection. When you help people, they help you. When you want a smack in the mouth? You smack someone. And if you want people to give you money? Share some of yours.

Think about it. If attachment hinders the flow of good things into your life, then the opposite of that would be unattachment—to the point where we give away some of what we value. What you give away will tend to come back to you.

I've had people tell me: "I've given all my life, and got nothing back." I don't think they were giving, I think they were *measuring*, and there's a difference.

WHAT ABOUT THOSE WEALTHY OLD MISERS WHO NEVER GAVE ANYBODY ANYTHING?

How often do we hear this kind of story ... "a penny-pinching old tightfist, who lived on bread crusts, dies with a million dollars parked under his bed?" It begs the question: "If you have to give in order to receive, what happened here?"

The balance in your bank book is not the measure of your abundance. Abundance is what's circulating through your life. Prosperity is a flow—giving and receiving. If you have a fortune in Swiss deposits, and you're not using it, then it's not enriching you. Technically it's yours, but in reality you're "receiving" nothing from it. It's not making you abundant and it might as well belong to someone else. So the principle of give and receive holds, even here.

IN A NUTSHELL

The trick to giving is to give without wanting anything back. If you expect something back, you are attached to a result—and when you are attached, less happens.

And should you enjoy your material possessions? Of course! Just make sure you own them and they don't own you.

ATTACHMENT TO LOVERS

"The origin of sorrow is desire."
Buddha

Mary is desperate for a man to love and adore her. Is there much hope of finding him? Not likely. Firstly, her desperation will push all the guys away. Secondly, while she's desperate, she's not so loveable.

Fred says to his girl: "I need you—and I can't live without you." But that's not love, it's hunger. You can't need someone desperately *and* love them at the same time. (And if you literally can't live without someone, you're a basket case! Who needs that?)

Loving people means giving them the freedom to be who they choose to be and where they choose to be. Love is allowing people to be in your life out of choice. Again, we're talking unattachment. To have something or someone, you let go.

ATTACHMENT—AND HATING THINGS . . .

"We cannot change anything unless we accept it."
Carl Jung

Hating things is a bad idea. While you hate something, you remain invisibly connected to it —so it will tend to hang around.

EXAMPLE: Let's say you are in debt and you hate it. That's a difficult position from which to improve your finances. You put so much energy into hating it that you stay stuck—you're drained. Once you accept your debt, free of the emotional turmoil, you can move out of it. Acceptance does not mean "giving up"—it means understanding what is.

EXAMPLE: Until you accept that you are overweight, you either: a) deny you are fat, or b) hate yourself for being fat. In either case, you stay fat. You only begin to lose weight once you accept you are fat.

When the Bible says, "resist not evil," it makes this point. Getting angry, or fighting doesn't work. You overcome what you don't like by accepting what is—not resisting—and replacing it with something positive.

V

WHAT YOU FOCUS ON EXPANDS . . .

so think about what you want!

"Sometimes I ask myself: 'Why am I the lucky one?'"

CHAPTER 5

Why Think Positive?
How Positive Thinking Shapes Your Subconscious
Thought Reaps Results

WHY THINK POSITIVE?

Imagine you are sitting in a jumbo somewhere over Europe, and an engine falls off the wing. How would you want the pilot to react? Would you want your pilot saying: "Stay calm and buckle up! This will be bumpy but we'll find a way home?"

Or would you want your captain running up and down the aisle yelling: "We'll all be killed! We'll all be killed?" Which fellow is more likely to get you down safely?

Now think about your everyday life in which you are your own pilot. Which approach is most likely to solve your problems: *"We'll find a way"* or *"We'll all be killed?"* This is the essence of positive thinking. It doesn't offer guarantees, but it gives you your best chance.

Losers focus on what's impossible until all they see is impossibility. Positive thinkers think about what's possible. In concentrating on the possibilities, they make things happen.

HOW POSITIVE THINKING SHAPES YOUR SUBCONSCIOUS

Our subconscious mind is a collection of all our thoughts. Our most common thoughts have created our strongest subconscious behaviors.

To understand positive thinking better, we need a picture of the subconscious. Imagine your brain as split into a top half and a bottom half, much like a large walnut. The top half is your conscious mind, containing your passing thoughts. The bottom half is your subconscious. In your subconscious are the various programs you were born with—like breathing and digestion—and programs you've created—like walking and talking.

Now, let's imagine you are learning to drive. Each time you approach a corner, you have a conscious thought in the "top" of your brain: "lift the right leg, move it six inches to the left, and press gently on the pedal." As you continue to have that *conscious* thought over a period of months, you develop an automatic program where you brake without thinking. The braking program has taken root in the bottom half of your brain— your subconscious. You have a new *subconscious* program.

This explains how, as an experienced driver, you can arrive home after driving for five hours—and say to yourself: "I don't even remember *driving* the car!" Your subconscious did the whole thing. ANY CONSCIOUS THOUGHT REPEATED OVER A PERIOD OF TIME BECOMES A PROGRAM.

So what happens if, for example, you have a conscious thought over a period of years ... "I'm always broke?" You develop an automatic program where you don't have to think. You can make yourself broke without any conscious effort.

How does this fit in with positive thinking? Simple. We have about 50,000 thoughts a day. For most of us, they are mainly negative thoughts: "I'm getting fat! I've got a bad memory. I can't pay my bills! Nothing I do ever works."

With mostly negative thoughts, what kind of subconscious behavior do we get? Mostly negative behavior—which sabotages our life and health without us even thinking.

People wonder why they end up broke and miserable, yet they have created their own automatic patterns through their repetitive thoughts. In the same way that we program ourselves to drive a car without thinking, we can program ourselves to be late, miserable or spend ourselves broke without thinking. And then we blame God.

Now here's what's exciting. When you understand about subconscious patterns, you realize that no one *has* to be a loser. Your future depends on your conscious thoughts. As you begin to discipline your mind, your new conscious thoughts create new subconscious programs. In the same way you can develop subconscious behavior to drive a car, you can develop subconscious behavior to be more successful. But it takes disciplined thinking ... and some *time.*

Now take Fred who attends a motivational seminar, and goes on a positive thinking kick. Fred says: "I'm going to turn my life around!" He writes out a few goals before breakfast ... "Get promoted, get a Rolls Royce, buy the Taj Mahal ... " and then spends the rest of the week in his usual negative spiral. By Friday he says: "I don't think this positive thinking stuff is working!"

He has perhaps moved from 48,000 negative thoughts per day to 47,500—and can't believe he hasn't won the lottery, cured his arthritis, and quit fighting with his wife.

Being positive for one day won't do it. Strengthening your mind is like strengthening your body. If you do twenty push-ups, and then race over to the mirror, you won't see any difference. Similarly, if you think positive for 24 hours, you will see little difference. But discipline your thinking for a few *months* and you will see even bigger changes in your life than you will ever see at the gym. Cleaning up our thinking is lifelong work. It is huge! It's made even harder because, often, we don't even know we are being negative when we're being negative.

If you want to check your thinking, check your life. Your prosperity, your happiness, the quality of your relationships, and even your health are a reflection of your most common conscious thoughts.

IN A NUTSHELL

Fred says: "I think like I do because my life is a mess!" No Fred, your life is a mess because you think like you do!

THOUGHT REAPS RESULTS

If there is something in your life you don't want, stop worrying about it and stop talking about it! The energy you put into it keeps it alive. Withdraw your energy and it goes away. An argument is the perfect example. If your husband comes home looking for an argument and you refuse to fight, what happens? He can't argue by himself!

Whenever you're worried about something—or embarrassed—or even just thinking about it, other people will keep talking about it. As a child this used to fascinate me. I could never understand why, whenever I had been smoking Dad's cigarettes, Mom would want to kiss me good night!

When you truly let go of something emotionally, it evaporates. This leads to another principle ... `

WHEN YOU LET GO OF THINGS, THEY LET GO OF YOU.

As long as you are defending yourself, people will attack you. Why? Because we only defend ourselves when we are unsure of our position. Really!

EXAMPLE—Let's say your neighbor accuses you of being a Martian from outer space. Would you leap headlong into an argument about aliens? No. You *know* you're not a Martian, so you would probably laugh.

EXAMPLE—Let's say you are the subject of office gossip. If you start issuing public statements and declaring your innocence, you'll fuel the fire. Ignore it and it will pass. Am I saying, don't defend yourself? I'm saying that while we protest and agonize, and jump up and down, we keep an issue alive.

I remember watching the protest marchers on TV in the 1960's. I asked Dad: "Why are they thumping each other?" He said: "Because they want peace!"

You don't fight war. You focus on peace.

IN A NUTSHELL

If you turn your life into a campaign *against* things, the things you fight will expand. Decide what you are *for.*

66

WE CHOOSE HOW WE SEE PEOPLE

Fred and Mary go on their first dinner date. Fred is determined to have a good time. Mary drops potato salad in her lap, and Fred says: "Here, let me help you wipe that up." She loses her house keys, and Fred says: "I do that all the time!"

Three years go by. Mary and husband Fred are out to dinner. She drops the potato salad in her lap. Fred says: "You're disgusting!" She forgets her keys. He says: "You bird brain!"

Same people, same circumstances, different attitude! We choose how we see people. When we *want* to like someone, we can be so tolerant. When we want to be irritated by people, we focus on their faults. It's not other people's behavior that determines how we feel about them—it's *our attitude.*

Most of us spend more time thinking about what's *wrong* than what's *right*: Mary has two mental lists about Fred. The first is the *wife's short list*—a brief inventory of Fred's shortcomings. The second is the *widow's long list*—a complete catalogue of Fred's qualities: his friendliness, his sense of humour, his generosity, his cute backside.

She spends her whole married life concentrating on the short list—the few things which irritate her ... "he leaves the newspaper spread all over the breakfast table," "he leaves the toilet seat up." Then one day poor Fred gets hit by a truck. Overnight she switches to the long list ... "Fred was such an angel ... kind, generous, hard working ... he was such a good husband."

If we want to have lists, shouldn't we at least do it the other way round?

67

Focus on all the things we adore about people, and when they're gone console ourselves with thoughts like "he snored anyway."

If I asked you: "What's wrong with your mother?" Wouldn't you find something? If I said: "List another five things you don't like about her appearance, her attitude, her behavior," could you do it? I bet you could. Given time you might think of a hundred things, or maybe a thousand. You might get to the point where you never want to see her again!

People who concentrate on the negatives usually defend themselves by saying: "I'm just being realistic." The fact is YOU CREATE YOUR REALITY. You choose how you see your mother, and everybody else. Take anybody in your life and concentrate on what you like about them, and your relationship will improve. It can be hard, and even scary, but it works.

GRATITUDE AND ABUNDANCE

"Show me one happy, ungrateful person!"
Zig Ziglar

All spiritual teachings encourage us to give thanks. Fred says: "Why should I spend my life satisfying God's ego?" Actually, I doubt God has an ego problem—when you can move mountains, make universes and do time travel, you don't need to prove anything!

We give thanks for *our* benefit, and here's why. We receive in life what we dwell upon. As we express gratitude for what we have, so we feel richer, and so more comes our way.

When I met my wife, Julie, I noticed that for all her beautiful qualities, she has one shortcoming. She can't add! But although she is never quite sure what she has earned, what she is owed and what she has spent, she has always enjoyed prosperity. Julie is a living demonstration that, as far as quality of life is concerned, *a sense of gratitude, and an inner knowing that life will bless you* is more important than logic and mathematics.

VI

FOLLOW
YOUR
HEART.

**Your mission in life
is not to be
without problems—
your mission is to
*get excited.***

CHAPTER 6

Doing What You Love
Your Career
Changing Direction
What's Your Excuse?

DOING WHAT YOU LOVE

"Don't go around saying the world owes you a living. The world owes you nothing. It was here first."
Mark Twain.

T here are two themes in this chapter:
1) You choose your attitude. If you want to, you can enjoy almost any job, and 2) If you work at something you love, you'll be happier, you'll be more likely to succeed and you'll probably make more money.

So first I say: *"Choose to like whatever you are doing at the moment."* Then I say: *"Go follow your heart."* Is there a contradiction here? No. In the short term, you often need to make the best of a situation. If you need the cash, you may need to stay with your current job while you plan your future. In the long term, you will only be fulfilled if you do what feels right for you.

PERFECT JOBS

It usually seems that other people's jobs are easier and more fun—and pay more! Nurses think doctors have it easy. Sales people think sales managers have it easy. Everyone thinks politicians have it easy. Eventually we discover there are no perfect jobs. Why? Because people only pay us to do things they can't, or don't want to do. If there were no problems to solve, our jobs wouldn't exist.

If you don't like your work, you have two options—CHANGE YOUR ATTITUDE or CHANGE YOUR JOB.

In daydreams, we say: *"If my job was easier, I'd be happy!"* but in reality, we don't like easy jobs. When work gets too easy, we usually leave! We relish challenge so much that we go looking for it, even in our leisure time. Why do you think golf is so popular? Because it's designed to drive you nuts.

Fred says: *"If I can get me a job that isn't repetitious, then I'll be happy!"* Most jobs are repetitious. If you are a secretary, you type one letter after another. If you are a movie star, you do one take after another. All repetition.

When we label parts of our life as "work" or "play," we limit ourselves. It's like we say: "I'm off to work now, so I expect to suffer until five o'clock." Instead of thinking "work" or "play"—think of it as all *your life*. Loving a job is like loving a person—you might be infatuated in the beginning, but "loving" long term is a decision you make.

GIVING YOUR BEST

"There is dignity in work only when it is freely accepted."
Albert Camus

There are two good reasons to do your best.

Firstly, when you give one hundred percent, you are happier. Remember back to when you were at school. Remember what it felt like walking to school, on those days when you had done *all* of your homework—and done your best. Didn't you feel just a bit more enthusiastic?

It doesn't matter whether you've been out of school for fifty years, the "homework principle" still applies. Your teachers told you to work hard, your parents told you to work hard, bosses tell you to work hard—but you don't work to please parents and teachers and to keep your boss off your back. You do it for you.

Secondly, the universe has a way of punishing laziness and arrogance. Enough things will go wrong in your life—and work—without you giving a half hearted effort. When we get casual, things start to collapse. Ask the boxer who underestimates his opponent. Ask the businessman who underestimates his competition. There's a word to describe giving it your best shot every time—it's called professionalism.

Have you ever noticed how some taxi drivers make a trip a pleasure, and some make it a pain? Same repetitious job. So where's the difference? Happy cabbies have a different philosophy. Fred says: "But good cabbies give good service because they're cheerful." No! They're cheerful *because* they give good service.

People who enjoy their work wake up saying: *"Today, I am going to be more effective and more caring than I was yesterday."* They don't always hit the bull's-eye, but it's their aim.

I recently spoke at a conference in Singapore with Mr. Zig Ziglar. Zig has been speaking professionally for over twenty-five years and he is internationally regarded as a man at the very top of his field. His busy schedule and sizeable speaking fees are testament to this.

Before his speech I said to him: "Zig, you must have given this talk a thousand times. How long did you prepare for today's presentation?" He said: "Three hours."

Despite his success, Zig takes no chances and no short cuts. He is committed to his craft and dedicated to constant improvement. To call Zig "talented" would be to underestimate the man, because it takes so much more than talent to stay at the top.

WHO DO YOU WORK FOR?

"Always do more than you are paid for, and one day you will be paid for more than you do."

Recently I was served by a rude waiter. His body language said something like: "Who gave you permission to come into this restaurant?" It took twenty minutes to get my cappuccino, and when it arrived, most of it was in the saucer. In conversation, I asked him about his job and his boss. He said: "I sure don't want to work for this turkey for the rest of my life."

Unfortunately, he had missed one major point about life in the workplace. YOU DON'T WORK FOR YOUR BOSS. YOU WORK FOR YOURSELF.

None of your employers will be perfect and your colleagues may be lazy. But when you sign on as an employee, your job is to give your best, not to pick holes in the guy who signs the checks.

When you only give fifty percent effort, you suffer much more than your boss. He only loses a few dollars. You lose your enthusiasm and your self esteem, and a whole chunk of your life.

IF I HAD A GOOD JOB ...

Some people believe that there are "happy" things to do and "unhappy" things to do. *Not so.* An interesting person can make a dull job interesting. This doesn't mean that an out-of-work banker ought to wash cars for twenty years—but a few months might be good therapy! With our affluence comes arrogance. The retrenched architect says: "I do buildings but I don't do windows." Dismissed executives attach themselves to the government nipple, never considering they might wait on tables rather than draw a dole check.

Enjoying your work is a choice. My brother, Christopher, knows how to make even lousy jobs memorable! If I had to pick someone to help me dig a ditch or paint a roof, or smash concrete, I would choose him. He just assumes it will be enjoyable.
You can have more fun plucking chickens with Chris than you have at some cocktail parties.

IN A NUTSHELL

You give your best not because you need to impress people. You give your best be-cause that's the *only* way to enjoy your work.

74

YOUR CAREER

This book is not a career guide. It is a philosophy of life—i.e. you have one life: spend it doing things you care about. To do this, you need to accept two ideas.

1. *"It's possible to do what you love—if not yet in your job, at least in your leisure time."* Some of us play the martyr, never putting time aside just for ourselves. If you can't do things you love in your leisure time, it's doubtful you'll ever allow yourself to work in a job you really love.

2. *"It's possible to be paid to do what you love."* Many of us grow up believing that work is meant to be a drag. Wrong! Millions of people have a ball at work and get paid for it.

Let us define what "doing what you love" is NOT. Doing what you love is not pulling in a pay check for lying on a tropical beach. It *is* having a passion for something—and putting all your love, energy and creativity into making it work. It *is* taking risks. And usually, it *is* having to make it work just so you can feed yourself!

The uncertainty is half the fun. When there is no struggle, there is something missing. That's why so many children of the rich and famous overdose on heroin and blow their brains out. They have no challenge. Whether they work or not, their material needs are met.

YOUR LIFE WILL ONLY WORK WHEN YOU TAKE FULL
RESPONSIBILITY FOR YOUR CHOICES. YOUR CHOICE
OF VOCATION IS AT THE TOP OF THE LIST.

Ask Fred: "Why are you doing this job?" He says: "Everybody has to be somewhere, doing something!" Not good enough, Fred. There are no medals for spending a lifetime doing something you hate. If you know in your heart that you are in the wrong kind of work, change your job. Do something you love.

I DON'T KNOW WHAT I WANT TO DO

If you don't know what you like doing, maybe you stopped listening to yourself years ago. Many of us became different people in order to please our family ... you wanted to play baseball *but* mother made you play piano, you dreamed of sports cars *but* always bought something "practical," you wanted to be a journalist but you became an accountant, you ached to travel South America *but* always vacationed at Uncle Ted's.

You took up "appropriate" hobbies. You did what was "expected." Then one day you woke up saying: "I don't know who I am, but I know I don't want to do this any more."

If you smother your passion for long enough, you won't even remember what you really love. A voice inside will remind you that it's selfish to do what you really want. That little voice might even be saying: "You hate your job and it serves you right."

It's also possible to *think* you like doing something because everybody expects you to like it. Here's what you notice when you *really* like doing something:

- It's easy to get out of bed in the morning and you never want to take a rest.
- You forget about time and you forget yourself.
- Effort is a minor consideration. You can talk about it for hours—and usually do!

HOW DO I REDISCOVER MY PASSION?

Simplify your life. Quit doing things out of habit. Eliminate some of the garbage from your routine so you can see more clearly. Switch off the TV for a month. Notice what you think about, notice what you read.

Listen to yourself. Next time a little voice inside says: "I love that, this excites me." LISTEN! Go to the city library, start at one end and walk to the other. Look at every shelf. What grabs you?

Try new things ... try oil painting, bonsai, coach a kids' soccer team, learn Italian. Try ten things and nine may not excite you, but number ten may open up a whole new world. If that doesn't work, try another ten things.

To find, you have to seek. If you have lost your life direction, you probably won't find it between drinks at the local bar. Give yourself a break, give yourself some time and space to examine what counts for you. Go to the mountains or the beach for a week *by yourself.* Fred says:

"I haven't got time for that." That's like saying "I'm lost—but I'm running so late, I can't look at a road map."

Most importantly, get comfortable with the idea of doing what you like. To do what you love doing, you have to believe it's possible. As you discover what you like to do with your time, you begin to find answers to the question, *"What do I want to do with my life?"*

IN A NUTSHELL

Many people don't know what they want—and they are upset because they are not getting it. If you don't know exactly what you want, figure out what is closest to it—and go from there.

TALENT

"Talent" doesn't have to mean you paint masterpieces. Caring for people is a talent. Teaching is a talent. Making people feel welcome is a talent. Solving problems is a talent. Managing is a talent. Parenting is a talent.

Too often we underestimate our own talents. The potter says: "If only I could make music, now *that* would be something." The pianist says: "If only I could make things with my hands … " Don't measure your abilities against others. Do what you can do. Accept what talents you have. Fulfillment comes from developing *your* gifts, not wishing for someone else's.

Mary says: "I have a God given talent with kids, but maybe I'm supposed to be a banker." If you are literally God's gift to pre-schoolers, why would he want you to be a number cruncher? Give him some credit! If you can figure out where your gifts are, he can too.

Another thing I notice: most people who tell you they have no talent haven't tried many things.

Having said this, talent is useful, but it isn't everything! When people talk about Jack Nicklaus' golfing success, they generally talk of his *extraordinary* talent. When Jack talks of his success, he talks about the *extra practice balls he hit.* Jack knew that the difference between Jack Nicklaus and a thousand other talented golfers was attitude and hard work.

Onlookers and underachievers put major emphasis on talent. For them, talent, or the lack of it, is a great excuse to do nothing. If there is an outstanding quality common to great artists, scientists, sports stars, humanitarians and business tycoons it is not their talent—it is their *focus.* Once you know what you want to do, get focused! You can't do everything. You can't save the whales, heal the sick and plug the ozone layer all at the same time. Leave some chores for the rest of humanity.

USE YOUR SPARE TIME!

"Work is love made visible."
Kahlil Gibran

Many people turn their hobby into their full time work, and the transition from "hobby" to livelihood is very often gradual ...

Frank loves photography and devotes his spare time to it. He photographs friends' weddings. He wins some local amateur competitions. Gradually, he gets more and more work. Within a couple of years he's making more money on weekends than at the office. Sure, some weddings get cancelled, some clients don't pay their bills, he has some lean months, but for Frank, it's all worth it.

Maria loves languages. She speaks Italian and English and decides to learn Spanish. She vacations in Barcelona. To improve her Spanish, she teaches South American migrants English after work—for free. Within two years, she's fluent in three languages. Maria applies for three travel jobs and misses out—but she doesn't quit. She does a translators' course to refine her skills. Finally she lands a position in a language school.

Jim loves hiking and camping, and has all the gear: boots, tents, rucksacks. He notices that some people want to camp, but they have no gear. He rents them his gear. Sometimes he organizes their whole camping trip, takes the people in his van—and charges them. Sometimes campers lose his ropes and burn his tents, but Jim reasons: "No job is perfect—it's better than my last job at the morgue!"

What do we learn from these people?

- That it is possible to make a living doing something you like.
- The world is a market place. Once you develop a skill, people will *pay* you for it.

Also we learn that real life is not like the soaps. TV goes like this—

- 7:30 p.m. Scene 1—Samantha decides to start a modeling agency.
- 7:34 p.m. Scene 2—Samantha rents an office the size of a tennis court.
- 7:36 p.m. Scene 3—Samantha appoints a manager and retires to Hawaii.

In real life Samantha would visit eight banks to get finance. In real life Samantha would work weekends in a hamburger joint. In real life Samantha would start out with an office the size of your bathroom.

Real life is more frustrating. Real life takes a little longer.

Speaking of soaps, people who turn pastimes into professions don't spend much time watching them. Living other people's lives is no match for living your own.

IN A NUTSHELL

If you want to earn a living doing what you love, your hobby is a possible source of income. Until you have leisure interests, you limit your options.

CHANGING DIRECTION

My father always did what he wanted to do. At different times he was a sailor, a butcher, a farmer, an inventor, a landscape artist and a real estate developer. I grew up believing that work was *whatever you wanted to do.* I assumed that whenever you wanted a different occupation, you started one. So whereas many people need courage to resist pressure from their parents and follow their dreams, I didn't. When I told my Dad: "I'm quitting law studies to become an artist!" he said: "If that's what you want to do, wonderful!"

I painted portraits until my mid twenties when I got excited about the benefits of "positive attitude." At that point I decided to make oil painting my hobby rather than my profession, and I began teaching personal development seminars for a living. Approaching thirty, I began writing books, and in order to illustrate my books, I became a cartoonist. I now spend most of my working time speaking to conferences and conventions.

I outline my own experience to explain in part why I wrote this book. It saddens me that more people don't see the possibility to do the work they love. To find meaning and excitement in your work, you have to follow your heart. I believe it, and I live it.

Of course, everybody doesn't want to be self employed. For some occupations, it's almost impossible to run your own business—you don't meet many self employed bank managers or jumbo pilots! And many people prefer to have one career rather than several. But I'm stunned that so many people actually get work that they hate, often with rather limp excuses! What I notice is that we choose careers that fit our belief system.

Many of us had our career path chosen by an ignorant teenager– ourselves! If you chose your first career at seventeen, maybe it's time to choose again. Consider having more than one career in your life.

Let's say you wanted to teach music, but you became an engineer to please your dad. Every day, Dad's words are ringing in your ears: "You've had opportunities I never had, I wish I could have built bridges." What should you do? Tune up the piano!

Firstly, *do it for your father's benefit:* You can't live your life through someone else. Dad has to find interest in his own life. While you are sacrificing yourself to please him, you are postponing his growth and yours. You are not here to fulfill the dreams of frustrated parents.

And do it *for your benefit:* Just because you spent four years becoming an engineer, why should you spend the next forty years doing something you hate? It's bad for your spirit, it's bad for your health and you are doomed to mediocrity!

Do you really have to love something to do it well? Did Beethoven love music? Did Ferrari like fast cars? Take two doctors. One is passionate about his patients. The other is passionate about his BMW. Which doctor would you choose to remove your gallbladder?

You say: "So should I quit my job at the post office and start a rock band?" Not without music lessons and a few gigs! There is such a thing as a calculated risk. You develop your abilities, you expand your knowledge, you study, you create a demand for your skills ... and then you move to doing what you love.

Fred says: "I've got a family to support. Do you want me to just quit the office?" Well Fred, if your heart is somewhere else, it seems a long term option.

WORKING FOR MONEY

"Many men go fishing all of their lives without knowing that it is not the fish they're after."
Henry David Thoreau

If you are working just for the money, you won't be happy and you probably won't make much money. It's the universe's way of prodding you to do something you really love.

In Chapter Four I talked about unattachment. When you really love what you do, you are less attached to money, and so you usually find you make more of it. Money is a game—you win by playing the game and not agonizing over the score.

You may appreciate money, but dedication goes way beyond money. Whatever work you are doing at the moment, *you are competing against people who love what they are doing.* If you don't love your work, you will be blown away by the competition.

Is there room for you? There's always room for excellence. Eighty percent of people are very nice, and also a bit mediocre. How often do you get picked up in a clean taxi? When did you last get to see your doctor on time? How often do you get fine service in a restaurant?

Doing what you love doesn't have to involve years of training and big expense—and it can often grow out of apparent disaster. Julie has a manicurist, Danielle, who used to rent a corner of a hairdressing salon. When the hairdresser doubled her rent, Danielle was devastated. Then she piled all her nail polishes into a fishing tackle box, and started doing home manicure visits on her motor scooter. She's punctual, gives great service and she's booked weeks ahead.

BUT IF I DID WHAT I LOVE, I COULD NEVER MAKE THE SAME MONEY I'M MAKING NOW

Doing what you love will very often offer you greater prosperity in the long term. But sometimes it won't. Sometimes, when you do what you love, you *need* less money.

Let's say you are a company president. You have a huge apartment, plus a weekender on a little farm, plus the fancy cars, plus the expense accounts that go with being a top executive. Your real love is breeding horses, and teaching horse riding, but you say: "I have to keep my job to maintain all this stuff!"

When you become a riding instructor, you might find that you don't need the penthouse and the sports cars. Sometimes we buy a lot of toys to take our mind off the fact that we hate our job. When you follow your heart, you might discover that one little farm and one little Jeep are enough.

IT'S NOT THE JOB ...

You'll notice something about good nurses—they like people even more than medicine.

There is a clue here about finding meaning in your career. THE JOB ISN'T IT! Whatever you do for a living is a vehicle to connect with people. Whether or not you are fulfilled depends on how you serve the *people.* Albert Schweitzer said: *" ... the only ones among you who will be truly happy will be those who have sought and found how to serve."*

Unfortunately, "serving people" sounds like slavery or sacrifice. It's not. It is simply knowing that there's joy in giving something of yourself that is uniquely yours. "Serving" can be teaching or nursing people. It can be selling them beautiful flowers, or repairing their radiators with a smile. It's not about your job description. It's about your philosophy.

Society often evaluates careers in terms of Ph.Ds and masters degrees, and we are in danger of missing the point. It's the people connections.

Let's say you are coaching a basketball team of twelve year olds. You might love basketball, and that's fine. But as soon as you understand that *it's not about basketball at all,* then you can really do something for those kids.

You might say: "Basketball coaches don't change the lives of twelve year olds." Wrong! Some do—and they are the coaches who understand they are teaching kids about life, and basketball is just the excuse.

Meanwhile, too many teachers tell themselves: "What do I matter? The kids don't care about algebra." Of course they don't! If you are teaching sixth grade, your mission is not algebra. It is children. If you are a banker, your mission isn't balance sheets, it's people.

"I DO!"

Some years ago, I was a guest author at Books and Co. bookstore, in Dayton, Ohio. As I was drawing cartoons in the store, the staff told me a romantic story about two of their customers ...

One day Rebecca Battles and Ray Cwikowski were browsing in the grief recovery section of the store. Ray and Rebecca had both recently lost their spouses to illness. They began talking and decided to attend some grief counseling sessions together. Ultimately, the two struck up a friendship.

Some months later, Rebecca was back at Books and Co. The assistant asked Rebecca: "Did you get what you wanted?" Rebecca said: "I got more than I dreamed of—I got the book I wanted and my fiancé, all in the same section! We're getting married on September 15th."

Books and Co. were so excited, they volunteered to hold the wedding reception in the bookstore! Bookshelves were moved, tables and chairs were hired, flowers were brought in, decorations were hung, and the gift wrap section became a restaurant.

Proprietors Annye and Joe stopped selling books and served wedding cake. It was a special and touching event.

Books and Co. are a living demonstration that joy comes from combining effort and imagination. It comes from choosing to be involved, and saying: "I can help." It would have been so much easier for Annye and Joe to say: "That's not our department. We're a bookstore. We don't do weddings."

Besides having fine books, Books and Co. invite jazz bands weekly. They hold poetry readings, fishing workshops and lectures. They even have pet days. The Sunday before I visited they had five hundred dogs in the store!

It's not *what* you do, it's *how* you do it. If you are a bookstore owner, or a boat builder or a baby sitter, you can either do what everyone else does, or you can use some imagination.

IN A NUTSHELL

The joy is in doing
your thing—and stretching
because you choose to,
not because you have to.

I DON'T CARE WHAT I DO,
SO LONG AS I GET RICH AND FAMOUS!

The Sanskrit word for "your purpose in life" is *dharma*. According to the *Law of Dharma*, we each have unique talents that we are here to discover. When we express those talents, we find joy. According to the law, we are most likely to discover those talents when we ask: "What can I give?" rather than: "What can I get?"

Bill Gates is one of the world's richest men. To hear him speak, it's obvious he is more excited by software than money. Elvis Presley didn't set out to make a fortune, he set out to make a record. Being rich is not a goal, it's a by-product.

As for fame, most famous people find it irritating and inconvenient. Why would you want armies of strangers climbing your back fence? What's the point in having fifty photographers across the street with telephoto lenses aimed at your bathroom window?

WHAT IF EVERYBODY DID WHAT THEY LOVED? WHO WOULD PATCH THE ROADS?

Although it may not be your calling, some people love patching roads ... no telephones, open air, big trucks, country music ... it has its advantages. Our neighbor Wolfgang is a surgeon. Recently, over a spaghetti Bolognese dinner, he told us about an exhilarating hemorrhoid operation he had performed that afternoon. As I tried to imagine myself operating on someone's backside, I thought: "Wolfie is a real comic!" And then I realized he wasn't joking. Wolfie is passionate about cutting people up—and he loves a good hemorrhoid. When Wolfie describes hemorrhoids, they come alive!

Different people like doing different things. We are all moving in different directions at a different pace. When you move to do what you love, there will be someone to step into your shoes.

IF I START DOING WHAT I LOVE WILL I HAVE LESS PROBLEMS?

No! Your mission in life is not to be without problems, your mission is to get excited!

Your best chance for prosperity is in doing what you love. Love is energy. Everything you do with love is infused with that "quality energy," and that kind of energy is more likely to translate into dollars. But that doesn't mean no frustration and no pain. I have a problem with some new age books that paint such rosy pictures. Their message is: "Just follow your dream and carry home the cash in a wheelbarrow."

IN A NUTSHELL

DOING WHAT YOU LOVE IS NOT A RECIPE FOR AN EASIER LIFE, IT IS A RECIPE FOR AN INTERESTING LIFE. MOST LIKELY YOU'LL TAKE ON MORE RESPONSIBILITIES AND MORE PROBLEMS!

"BEING HAPPY!"

When I took the manuscript of my first book, "BEING HAPPY!" to publishers, they all said: *"The last thing the world needs is another self improvement manual."* They also said that, to be writing books like "BEING HAPPY!", I should be a psychiatrist—except for one fellow, and he thought I should see one!

But after a year and a half of rejections I found Media Masters, a publisher with a vision, in Singapore. Media Masters soon told me that the book market is extremely competitive, and that newspapers and TV have little interest in unknown authors. We needed a strategy.

We decided to take "BEING HAPPY!" direct to the people. When we launched the book in Singapore, I took my easel and microphone into almost every book store in the city. I drew my cartoons, talked about my philosophies and signed books. In the high schools and universities I talked to the students, and in the corporations, I talked to the staff. We stuck with this plan until "BEING HAPPY!" hit the Singapore bestseller lists, and then we used the same strategy in Malaysia, then Australia, and so on.

I spent six years traveling countries all over the globe. I spoke in warehouses and prisons, and cartooned in a thousand shopping centers—my next book should be "Shopping Malls of the World." For the most part I reveled in the project. But there were days when I would wake up in some hotel room and think: "If I go into another book store I'll vomit!"

One book store at a time, one city at a time, one country at a time, we took "BEING HAPPY!" to the international marketplace. And gradually, the newspapers and TV stations began to call us!

We had some fun along the way. We did a whole promotional tour of Australia during an airline strike. In New Zealand, they had me drawing cartoons on radio!

To launch "BEING HAPPY!" in America, we organized a cocktail party for the media at the Australian Embassy on Fifth Avenue in Manhattan. We sent out invitations to what seemed like every newspaper, news bureau, TV station and radio station on the East Coast of the U.S.A. We catered for two hundred people. I flew to New York for the launch on June 20th, 1990.

As it happened, June 20th was the day a fellow called Nelson Mandela also flew to New York. How many media people thought little Andrew was bigger news than Nelson Mandela? Zero.

If you have ever had a cocktail party by yourself, just you and eleven waiters, you'll know that the service is unforgettable.

People ask me: "What did you do to sell a million books?" I tell them: "I flew a million miles, gave five hundred speeches, a thousand interviews—and lost my baggage twenty-three times!"

This story is not about books or business—it's about any successful project you care to name. You start wherever you can. You do everything you can. It's more about effort than luck.

PASSION

When you care about what you do, enthusiasm carries you through. When you are passionate, no one else has to motivate you.

If you open your "dream restaurant," and no one comes to eat, you keep trying new recipes, ideas, and locations until the place is crammed. If you run out of money first, you take your enthusiasm to someone who has more money than you—and you get a partner. You go through frustrations—and a few chefs—but in your heart, you know you're on course. Sure you need plenty of determination, but your passion is your foundation.

Vitality comes from a sense of purpose. You owe it to yourself and you owe it to other people to do what excites you. There are already enough lukewarm people in the world who get burned out without ever having been on fire.

Following your dream is no guarantee of an easy ride. Life usually becomes more challenging, but you embark on an outer journey that starts the inner journey. You have a chance to blossom—to see who you really are.

IN A NUTSHELL

WHEREVER YOU ARE,
YOU AREN'T *STUCK*—YOU
ARE A HUMAN BEING,
NOT A TREE!

"WHAT'S YOUR EXCUSE?"

You may have read this chapter with a touch of irritation, thinking: "Andrew, it's fine to do what you love but you don't know my situation."

If you have unfulfilled dreams, analyze your excuses. Usually we are not very honest with ourselves. We say things are *impossible* when the truth is, they're very *inconvenient.*

Mary says: "I would really love to study archaeology—but of course it's impossible." What she really means is: "to study archaeology, I would need to either: a) get the necessary entry qualifications: b) waitress part time at Greasy Joe's: c) get a loan: d) stop going out to dinner for four years: or e) all of the above."

She decides that archaeology is not worth that kind of effort. In fact, Mary says: "If you think I'd go through all that, you've got rocks in your head!"

Jim says: "I would love to own my own little apartment." He has been saying the same thing for twenty-three years. What Jim means is: "I'd love to have my own apartment if: a) I didn't have to save any harder: b) I didn't have to work harder: or c) I didn't have to live where apartments are cheaper." Jim keeps renting.

Mary and Jim have made understandable decisions that are neither right nor wrong, and that's fine. What is destructive is when they pretend they had no choice.

How many people swear it's impossible to change careers—until a heart attack convinces them otherwise? Either we call the tune, or circumstances and other people call it for us. WHY WAIT FOR A DOCTOR TO TELL YOU YOU'VE GOT SIX MONTHS LEFT BEFORE YOU START DOING WHAT YOU LOVE IN LIFE?

WHAT IF MY DREAM IS IMPOSSIBLE?

Humans do incredible things. Consider Roger Crawford, the American born with one leg and two arms, but no hands. Roger became a professional tennis player. That is, he earned professional status and coached tennis for a living. You can read his story in his book, "Playing from the Heart." Roger's story makes you take a second look at your limitations.

Digital Dan, of Ferndale, California, was a carpenter until he got cancer of the throat and had his voice box removed. When he could no longer speak, he became a disc jockey! Dan types his words into a laptop computer, and the laptop does the talking!

There is a pattern amongst people who achieve their dreams—they often start from a long way behind. You find sickly asthmatics who became champion athletes, you find tycoons who were bankrupts. You find a thousand stories of illiterate immigrants who became college professors and company presidents.

When the odds are stacked against you, you develop a mental toughness just to survive. The strength you develop to survive becomes your secret weapon.

IN A NUTSHELL

We always have choices. If you are not doing something, it's because you are putting your energy elsewhere. The question is not: "Why is this impossible?" The question is: "What am I unwilling to do?"

When you say: "I'll do this thing. I don't care how hard it is," life then starts to support you.

90

VII

GOD IS NEVER GOING TO COME DOWN FROM A CLOUD AND SAY: *"YOU NOW HAVE PERMISSION TO BE SUCCESSFUL!"*

You have to give yourself permission.

ANDREW MATTHEWS

CHAPTER 7

Make a Start!
Courage
Trying New Things
The Secret of Power
Why Not You?

MAKE A START!

"A man of knowledge lives by acting, not thinking about acting."
Carlos Casteneda

"You can't build a reputation on what you're GOING to do."
Henry Ford

Has this ever happened to you? You are sitting at your desk—either at home or at work—and the phone rings. The caller asks you to write down his number. You apologize: "Just a minute while I find something to write with." Searching for a pencil, you start rotating stacks of junk around your desk ... piles of medical receipts, airline tickets, insurance policies, pizza cartons, nose drops, coffee cups and old newspapers. "Sorry to keep you waiting, there's a pencil here somewhere ... "

You plough into the drawers amongst flashlight batteries, tooth picks, golf tees, weight loss brochures, wedding photos, loose change from Hong Kong, a kid's crayon. A crayon! You scribble the number in lemon yellow and hang up.

You think to yourself: "Now that I've found those insurance policies, I'll put them into a folder." Then you file the airline tickets under "travel" and the coffee cups in the dishwasher. Before you know it, you're on a roll ... erasers into the top drawer, telephone books onto the shelf, pizza cartons into the bin. You even wipe the chocolate caramel off the telephone.

Suddenly you have a vision ... "I could have a *tidy* office." You feel a surge in your chest and you begin to plan: "I'm going to make fresh files with color coded labels, I'll have a special jar for ball-points. I'll even empty my waste basket every week!" Now you're on a mission that's bigger than writing utensils. You're creating the world's cleanest workspace! By midnight you've found a dozen pencils, but does it matter? No! You're having too much fun with the vacuum cleaner.

This is the *office cleaning principle*, and it applies to writing reports, digging ditches, doing your tax, washing the car. You get excited about doing things *after* you start. You take the plunge, and *then* you feel the energy and excitement.

We often make the mistake of saying: "When I get the energy, I'll begin jogging every morning!" No! You start first. "When I feel more enthusiastic, I'll do my homework." Wrong. "When I get the energy, I'll start my own little business!" No!

You get the energy and the enthusiasm for the job *after* you begin. You get the energy as a result of your involvement. The secret is to *make a start*.

Another thing about starting things ... you will never ever be absolutely *ready* for anything! For example, a public speech? Are you ever one hundred percent prepared for a speech? No. No matter how many times you rewrite it, no matter how long you spend learning it, you will be telling yourself: "If only I had a little more time ... " Take marriage. Are you ever ready for the walk down the aisle? Are you ever totally prepared for what follows? Not likely. You prepare as best you can, and then you take a deep breath and jump in.

Fred says: "Give me some kind of guarantee that I won't fail. Then I'll start." No Fred. You commit to do something. You prepare as best you can, and then you *start without all the answers and without any guarantees.*

IN A NUTSHELL

You get motivated by doing things, not thinking about them. Action gets you excited and action reveals opportunity. Take the plunge.

GET SERIOUS

All the motivators and psychologists say you have to "believe in yourself." That makes sense. But before you can *believe in yourself*, you have to *believe yourself*.

So many people are wimps when it comes to promises and commitment. They say they'll do something, and they don't. They promise they'll help you, and they go fishing. They promise they'll pay their bills, and they leave the country! Then they wonder why their life doesn't work.

Only commit to something if you know you will follow through. If necessary, make less promises and less commitments, but *whatever you say you'll do, do it*. Gradually your word becomes law for you—and that's when you really believe in yourself.

COURAGE

"Comfort starts as a servant and becomes a master."
Kahlil Gibran

People write songs about singing in the rain, but in real life, when they get wet, they moan. People love to watch Indiana Jones wading knee deep through snakes and spiders—but when their office air conditioning fails, they explode. Perhaps if we had less adventure on our video recorders we would look for more adventure in everyday life.

"Being comfortable" is overrated. I'm not talking about "money" comfortable—I'm talking "situation" comfortable. Much of our stress is created by our addiction to comfort ... "planes should always be *punctual*, the workload should always be *easy*, the bank overdraft should be *comfortable.*"

Too much comfort gets boring. Our brains seize up! The less rules you make for how life ought to be and how you ought to feel, the easier it is for you to respond to whatever happens.

If you follow any kind of dream you'll sometimes be uncomfortable— you'll get rejected, criticized, short of cash and exhausted. When adversity comes your way, see it as part of the process. Be fascinated. Be interested. Be amused. See the fun in being behind the eight ball.

"Get off your backside and do something!"

Something else about comfort. You'll notice that, very often, *courage* is better rewarded than *IQ*—and this frustrates some people. Fred says: "I'm highly intelligent, I've got two degrees—and I can't believe that less intelligent people get better jobs and make more money!" As a rule, rewards come when we risk our reputation or our money—or both.

IN A NUTSHELL

Courage is not the absence of fear—courage is acting in spite of fear. People who do *nothing* with their lives are just as scared as people who take *major risks*. It's just that the first group get scared over *tiny things*. Why not get scared over something significant?

"Have you learn'd lessons only of those who admired you,
and were tender with you?
Have you not learn'd great lessons from those who reject you,
and brace themselves against you?"
Walt Whitman

The temptation is to surround ourselves with friends and colleagues who tell us what we want to hear. Then, when things are falling apart, we've got someone who'll say: "It's not your fault!" There's value in having people who will challenge us—it's just less comfortable.

TAKE A STAND

"If you feel you are getting screwed, you probably are!"
Chin-Ning Chu

"Following your heart" doesn't mean being *soft*. The world is a tough place and nature's laws are severe. The weak lamb gets eaten by the fox. Weak people get eaten too! When you are weak, the foxes see you as an easy target—and you get picked on and you get stung.

> One day a frog was sitting by a stream. A scorpion came by, and said: "Mr. Frog, I would like to cross the stream, but I am a scorpion and cannot swim. Would you be so kind as to swim across with me on your back?"
> And the frog said: "But you are a scorpion and *scorpions sting frogs!*"
> Said the scorpion: "Why would I sting you? I want to get to the other side!"
> "OK," said the frog, "climb on my back and I will take you."
> They were just halfway across the stream when the scorpion stung the frog. Writhing in agony, and with his last breath, the frog said: "Why did you do that? Now we'll both drown!"
> "Because," said the scorpion, "I am a scorpion, and *scorpions sting frogs!*"

Look out for scorpions! There are people around who don't mind drowning if they can drag you down too.

Some people are to be avoided. Sometimes you have to stand and fight. When do you make a stand? You can only ask yourself: "What do I feel is fair?" Then take your position, irrespective of whether other people are going to like you or think you are nice.

You can wear yourself out trying to get everyone to like you, or agree with you, and in the end, *they don't like you* and *you don't know who you are*.

Ultimately, you can only depend on your inner guidance—in other words, follow your own heart.

TRYING NEW THINGS

"If you do what you've always done, you'll get what you've always gotten."

Ask "courageous" people how they find the nerve to quit jobs, start businesses, buy real estate, move to different countries, do anything new, and you'll find a common approach. They ask themselves the question: "IF THE WORST HAPPENED, COULD I DEAL WITH IT?" When the answer is: "Yes," they take the plunge. It's the secret for the big risks and small risks ...

EXAMPLE: Ted is unsure about buying an apartment. He asks: "What's the worst that could happen?"

Answer: "I could lose my job and be forced to sell the apartment at a loss. I might lose my savings, and have to start all over again." He says to himself: "Starting over would be frustrating but I'd somehow handle it." He buys.

EXAMPLE: Ian wants to ask Jane for a date. He asks himself: "What's the worst that could happen?"

Answer: "She might throw her Coke in my face." Ian says: "I'm used to that sort of treatment! I'll ask!"

EXAMPLE: Louise wants to quit medicine to study archaeology. She asks: "What's the worst that could happen?"

Answer: "My father might hit the roof, my friends might say I'm crazy, I might have to study twice as hard." She says: "If the worst happened, I'd survive it."

IN A NUTSHELL

It is not a negative approach to ask: "What is the worst that could happen?" It is a way of measuring your commitment. Break your vague fears into specific possibilities, and risk taking becomes more fun.

THE SECRET OF POWER

When an archer shoots for nothing,
he has all his skills.
If he shoots for a brass buckle,
he is already nervous ...
The prize divides him.
He cares.
He thinks more of winning
than of shooting—
and the need to win
Drains him of power.

Chuang Tzu

MATTHEWS

If you have ever swung a bat or kicked a goal, you will know that sport is more than a game. And you will know why grown adults—accountants, truck drivers, brain surgeons and check-out clerks—spend weekends in the blazing sun and the pouring rain, playing ball. At the ping pong table, on the badminton court, on the ski slopes, you can educate yourself about the laws of life. More than great fun, sport teaches us about our personal power. Some of the things we learn ...

Live in the present moment. It is possible to think too much. You bowl your best ball, throw your best pitch, shoot your best shot when you forget about the score. The less you worry about winning and about what other people think, the better you perform.

Forcing things never works. Real power comes when you are relaxed. Try clubbing a golf ball down the fairway with brute strength! You are most powerful when you are not trying to prove you are powerful! This also applies to people management.

Keep your cool. Getting angry never works. Have you ever seen a golfer get angry? He's history. What about irate boxers and race car drivers? Dead meat! The same goes for parents and school teachers.

Don't hate your opponent—lift your performance! Hating things and people drains your energy and takes your mind off what you are meant to be doing.

If you think the world is against you, it is. Blaming other people doesn't work. Once you decide that everything is going wrong—that the umpires, the referees, the wind and the ball are trying to ruin your life, they will. Successful athletes are like any other effective people—they take maximum responsibility. They don't blame their mother.

Extraordinary performance stems from extraordinary commitment. The casual observer assumes that a Michael Jordan or a Steffi Graf was simply born with more talent. But many people are born gifted. A closer look reveals that the stars demand more of themselves than anybody else.

In sport and life you must concentrate on what you want. When you think about what you *don't* want to happen, e.g. a double fault, a slice into the water hazard, a dropped catch, it happens! Why? Your mind works on pictures. You tell yourself: "*Don't hit the ball into the net!*" You get a mental picture of the ball going into the net. You tell yourself: "*I don't want that!*" Your mind creates a picture of the bad shot. It then goes to work with the only mental picture it has—a picture of a ball in the net. And you make it happen!

   Fear is a killer, not just in sport, but during a job interview, during a speech, during anything where you want to perform. When you concentrate on what you fear, and create those disaster pictures in your head, you are heading for disaster. Concentrate on what you want.

IN A NUTSHELL

   All children should have a chance to play some sport—not for the trophies they get, but for the lessons they learn. Not the least of these is, *it's not where you start, it's how you finish.*

WHY NOT YOU?

"When I was young I thought that people at the top really understood what the hell was happening ... whether they were cardinals or bishops or generals or politicians or business leaders. They knew. Well, I'm up there, and now I know they don't know."
David Mahoney

When I was a kid, we used to visit family friends, the Zerners. They always had Coca-Cola in their refrigerator. (Mom said it was because they were rich. At home, we drank water.) So I figured once you had Coke at your house, you had really "made it." Then one day we got some Coke in our refrigerator. Only then did I realize Coca-Cola didn't make you a superstar.

For a while it seemed to me people who wore suits had really "made it." Dad only wore suits to funerals, and I figured that didn't count. Then gradually it dawned on me that wearing a suit didn't make you a genius.

When I was twelve, I wanted to be Prime Minister of Australia. "Prime Ministers would know it all!" That idea more or less took care of itself.

Until I started writing books, I thought authors must have all the information.

Maybe, at times, you have thought the same—that there are *experts* who have all the answers. *There aren't.* Successful people aren't superhuman. They have one brain, twenty-four hours in the day, and usually, two arms and legs. They have developed skills and disciplines and taken them to the market place. You can develop your own skills and disciplines and take them to the market place.

IN A NUTSHELL

Nobody is born with special permission to succeed. God doesn't come down from a cloud and say: "Now is your time!" He doesn't say: "You can," or "You can't." YOU DO!

WHEN THE STUDENT IS READY...

"When the student is ready, the teacher will appear."

When you are absolutely committed to changing your life or reaching a goal, the *means* to help you get there present themselves—people show up, friends lend you books, advertisements "jump out and hit you," you find yourself in the right place at the right time ...

Am I saying you are more aware of opportunities, or that you literally *attract* opportunities? It's both.

I remember on October 19, 1983, I made a decision that, whatever it took, I was going to be a much happier person than I had been for my first 25 years. Three days later, for no reason at all, I tuned into a radio station I never listened to, and heard about a coming seminar. I attended that course and it was a turning point in my life.

My experience is not uncommon—it's more the norm. The key is commitment. Commitment is not wishing for something—it is a decision deep within yourself to do whatever it takes.

IN A NUTSHELL

ONCE WE MAKE A DECISION TO DO A THING, THE MEANS APPEAR. We might explain away these lucky breaks as coincidence. But with keen observation, we notice it happens regularly.

VIII

WHEN YOU
FIGHT LIFE,
LIFE ALWAYS
WINS.

**If you want
more peace of mind,
stop labeling
everything that happens
as "good" or "bad."**

"I can't help it—I come from a family of worriers!"

CHAPTER 8

Luck
Thoughts
Peace of Mind
The Whole Picture

LUCK

There once lived a farmer. He had a son and a horse. One day the farmer's horse ran away, and all his neighbors came to console him, saying: "What bad luck that your horse has run away!" And the old man replied: "Who knows if it's good luck or bad luck."

"Of course it's bad luck!" said the neighbors.

Within a week, the farmer's horse returned home, followed by twenty wild horses. The farmer's neighbors came to celebrate, saying: "What good luck that you have your horse back—plus another twenty!"

And the old man replied: "Who knows if it's good luck or bad luck!"

The next day the farmer's son was riding amongst the wild horses, and fell and broke his leg. The neighbors came to console him, saying: "What bad luck!"

And the farmer said: "Who knows if it's good or bad luck!"

And some of the neighbors were angry, and said: "Of course it's bad luck, you silly old fool!"

Another week went by, and an army came through town, enlisting all the fit young men to fight in distant lands. The farmer's son, with his broken leg, was left behind. All the neighbors came to celebrate, saying: "What good luck that your son was left behind!"

And the farmer said: "Who knows?"

We can spend our whole lives figuring everything out. "This is good, that is bad ..." It is futile. We label events as "disasters" when we only see one percent of the picture.

So long as you believe that everything is going wrong, it will keep going wrong. As long as you go through your day kicking and screaming, nothing works. But the minute you change your point of view, *everything* changes.

You are bumped off a plane and you say: "This is terrible. I'm in a hurry. People are waiting for me. I have to be on that flight." While you stay with that thought pattern, people will trip over you, spill coffee in your lap and lose your baggage. WHEN YOU FIGHT LIFE, LIFE ALWAYS WINS.

Things will improve the minute you say: "There are no accidents in my life. I am where I am meant to be." You meet an old friend, you make a new friend, you take time to read a book and life begins to improve.

Taking the logical point of view doesn't always work. You apply for a job, and miss out. If you tell yourself: "That was *my* job. I had the qualifications and the experience and now my life is ruined," you can be a wreck. You can be a wreck for a week or if you want, a lifetime. You can argue your case with wonderful logical reasoning. Your argument will work but your life won't, because life isn't logical!

If you want more peace, stop labeling everything that happens as good or bad! In his book "The Frogship Perspective," Dean Black quotes two true stories:[2]

"A sixteen year old all-star basketball player loses both legs in a farming accident."

"A middle aged man gains sight after being blind since birth."

The basketballer, Curt Brinkman, becomes an outstanding wheelchair athlete. Interviewed, Curt says: "I'd just as soon be in the situation I'm in now as have legs. I don't know what I'd be like if I still had my legs ... I know what I've done. I know what I want to do. And it's exciting. There's no way I'd want to see it any different."

And the fifty-two year old man who has his sight restored by a surgeon's knife ..." As a blind man he had gotten on very well," says his psychologist Richard Gregory. "But when he finally could see, his previously remarkable achievements seemed paltry and his position almost foolish."

The man finds seeing a great disappointment and dies depressed within a year.

THOUGHTS

In simplest terms, we have two ways of looking at the world:
- The world is a mess.
- The world is OK as it is.

"THE WORLD IS A MESS"

It takes so much energy to find fault with everything, agonizing that some people cheat and steal, that some people are lazy, that some people eat too much and some spend too much, that some people get caviar and some get beans. And criticizing makes you miserable too.

We might point to the starving in Calcutta as if to say: "Everything is going wrong." That can be an excuse for not making our own life work. If you are an Indian—or if you're living in Calcutta and helping the Indians, perhaps the situation makes a little more sense. But to judge situations we don't fully understand from a distance isn't helpful. If you want to make a difference, and do something about it, that's another matter. But agonizing doesn't help. The Mother Teresa's of the world don't agonize—they *act*.

"THE WORLD IS OK AS IT IS"

The alternative option is to accept the world as it is. You say: "What is the evidence to suggest that the world is fine?" Because it is the way it is! The moon rolls around the earth and the earth rolls around the sun, roses bloom, birds sing, people marry ...and divorce, neighbors fight. It's all part of the grand scheme of things.

To say: "People shouldn't get sick, people shouldn't tell lies." That is like saying: "The sun is too big!" Things work the way they are.

Mary says: "I'll never be happy until there is world peace." That may seem noble, but it's not very intelligent! Better to be happy in the meantime—and work at making your little corner of the world more peaceful. It is possible to accept the world as it is and still accept a share of responsibility to improve things.

IF NOT FOR THIS, I'D BE HAPPY!

A retired executive told me: "I used to worry about million dollar take-overs. Now I get stressed out over dirty windows and lawn clippings!" He said: "Now that I have less major worries, I worry about minor things that don't matter."

It's true. We *find* things to worry about. Picture yourself on a twelve hour plane trip. You've just taken off, and you are hoping to relax and maybe even get some sleep. And then you notice it. The fellow next to you is sniffing, and he's doing it like clockwork, every six seconds. "One, two, three, four, five, *sniff*, one, two, three, four, five, *sniff* ..." Oh no! This guy's a sniffing metronome!" You say to yourself, "If I didn't have to put up with this turkey, I'd be happy!"

You take out your calculator—"Ten sniffs a minute multiplied by ...that's seven thousand two hundred sniffs until Frankfurt. This could be the worst night of my life!"

Until now you hadn't noticed the sleeping baby behind you. But now he's wide awake and testing his lungs. Non stop howling infants on non stop flights are hard to ignore. This is when you say to yourself: "And I was worried about 'Sniffer!' I can tolerate bad manners, but wailing babies? No wonder I'm upset!"

It's about now that things take a turn for the worse. Without warning your jumbo jet shudders and plunges earthward. You feel the blood drain from your face as your stomach lodges in your throat. Everyone is screaming. Reaching for your life jacket you make a deal with God: "Get me out of this power dive and I'll never be irritated by sniffers again. I'll happily suffer screaming infants all the way to Europe."

The plane levels out and begins to climb. The captain apologizes for the unexpected turbulence. Baby stops crying and Sniffer falls asleep. You resume your crossword in peace—and guess what! Sniffer starts to *snore.* "Oh no! If I didn't have to put up with this, I'd be happy!"

Here's how life is. We have a "worry hierarchy" and the most important things get worried about. While we've got a broken leg we don't worry about a headache—until the broken leg has healed. Snoring husbands only irritate us until the bedroom catches fire.

So how do we get less irritated? We recognize that our stress is caused by rules in our own head. As soon as we relax some of the rules, or drop them altogether, we don't get so annoyed when the real world ignores our rules.

We can make a conscious decision: "No one is going to ruin my day." We make a pact with ourselves that "no arrogant bank clerk, no parking meter attendant, no traffic cop, no waitress with a chip on her shoulder is going to mess with my 24 hours." We remind ourselves that in the context of world events, a confrontation with a rude checkout clerk is not *that* dramatic.

IN A NUTSHELL

There are alternatives to getting angry. It is possible to be fascinated or amused. The less rules you have about how life ought to be, and how other people ought to behave, the easier it is to be happy.

MATTHEWS

WHY SHOULD I LEARN TO CONTROL MY THOUGHTS?

For two reasons:
- You can't control your environment, the weather or other people's opinions about you. The one thing over which you have total control—and the most important—is your thoughts.
- Externals don't make us happy!

I say: *"If I had 'X' I'd be happy!"* Wrong. I'd be happy for about twenty-four hours, and then find something else to bitch about ... I pray for a new Porsche, and it falls out of the sky. I'm ecstatic. I drive it to the supermarket where some kid attacks it with a shopping cart ... Now I'm saying: *"I won't be happy until I catch the little punk!"*

Recall an incident in the last week that disturbed you: you were abused in traffic, your boyfriend forgot your birthday, your wallet was stolen. Realize it wasn't the incident that was disturbing, it was your thoughts about it. You say: "*Anybody* would have been upset." Wrong. Most people. All our lives we've been conditioned to think certain thoughts about things. It's the thoughts that make us unhappy—and we can change our thoughts.

IN A NUTSHELL

You improve your quality of life by working on your thoughts, and your thoughts affect your feelings.

PEACE OF MIND

WHY DO I WANT PEACE?

Most people agree they want more love in their life, but why work at peace of mind? Because LOVE AND PEACE ARE INSEPARABLE. Love is not an emotion. Love is not "owning" a girlfriend or boyfriend. Love is experiencing without judgement. If you look for love, you'll find more peace—and if you look for peace you'll find more love.

Peace is not Valium. Peace is *balance*.

Lesson one for martial artists is balance. In karate you learn that your power depends on balance and a still mind. Get too excited and you're a dead duck. Golfers know about balance. At the tee, furious swings count for zero. Instead, you relax, sense your power, clear your head of the chatter, and bingo—it all comes together.

Balance, or peace of mind, is your source of power. Peaceful doesn't mean sleepy! Peaceful means aligning with forces rather than fighting them. Peaceful means seeing the broader picture and not getting hung up on details.

AS SOON AS I PAY OFF THE CAR, I'LL BE MORE PEACEFUL.

Fred says: "Let me take care of all the bills and *then* I'll look for some peace." Sounds good in theory, but the results are usually disappointing. This is because our main mission in life is not to eliminate the mortgage and extend the swimming pool.

We are here to help one another. Because of this, the universe gives us the following cues:

- WE ARE HAPPIEST WHEN WE ARE HELPING OTHER PEOPLE WITH THEIR LIVES.
- WE ARE LONELIEST WHEN OUR PRINCIPLE GOAL IS OUR OWN PERSONAL SECURITY.

And if you want absolute security in this life, you chose the wrong planet.

Fred says: "If I can get my little house in the suburbs and if I can get a nest egg for my retirement, I'll be secure." Sure, Fred. Try telling that to a runaway bus at an intersection! Your only security is within yourself—security anywhere else is a myth. Banks collapse, companies disappear, jumbo jets fall out of the sky.

So how do you deal with the uncertainty of life? You accept it. Enjoy it. You say: "Half the fun of being here is knowing that anything could happen next." You make an agreement with yourself: "Whatever happens, I'll handle it." You look fear in the face. You say: "If my house burns down, I'll move. If I get fired, I'll quit! If I get hit by a bus, I'm out of here." End of story.

This isn't flippant. It's realistic. Earth is a dangerous place. Lots of people die here! That doesn't mean you have to live life like a frightened rabbit.

SO HOW DO I GET PEACE OF MIND?

It's partly attitude. It's partly developing the daily habit to relax your mind.

You'll notice something about people who have peace of mind: they each have a daily discipline for maintaining equilibrium. Many pray, some meditate, some walk on the beach at dawn. Each find sanctuary and silence. In going inside themselves, they see outside of themselves.

For four years I ran weekend seminars, teaching mind and body relaxation. I continued to be amazed at the changes in people who learned to really relax. They would report: "My headaches have gone." "My backache has disappeared." "Business has prospered." "The children are happier." "My husband is behaving." "My golf has improved." For the most part, the participants hadn't "done" anything. They had simply let go.

In the western world, we are taught to "do" things. I have no argument with that. But before we start *doing anything*, we have to stop *fighting everything*. We grow up believing in struggle. We learn to force things and push people. We wear ourselves out and we screw it up.

I learned about this the hard way. When I set out to be a portrait

artist, I decided nothing would get in my way. My recipe was "paint ten hours a day, seven days a week—and if that doesn't work, paint all night." I painted some woeful pictures. Exhausted and frustrated, it began to dawn on me that desperation doesn't work.

Life remains a struggle while you insist it's a struggle. There is such a thing as letting things unfold.

A young boy traveled across Japan to see a great martial artist. Given an audience with the Sensei, he said: "I want to be the best in the land. How long will it take?"

And the Sensei said: "Ten years."

The student said: "Master, I am very keen. I will work day and night. Now how long will it take?"

And the Sensei said: "Twenty!"

MINDFULNESS

Most of us have discovered how hard it is to live in the present, and much of our time is spent either regretting the past or fearing the future.

Living in the moment is like walking a tightrope. You're bound to fall off, but with practice, you manage to keep your balance longer and longer. Here are two strategies to keep your mind on the present:

113

- TAKE AS MUCH TIME AS YOU NEED TO DO EVERYTHING YOU DO

Refuse to live life in a hurry. When our belief system says: "There is never enough time," guess what! *There never is enough time.* We run for the bus, we run for the elevator, we eat lunch between phone calls.

Whatever you have to do, tell yourself: "While I'm writing this letter, (ironing this shirt, pumping these weights), my full attention is on what I'm doing. *How long it takes is how long it takes.* I refuse to hurry."

- PRACTICE "DOG AWARENESS"

Take your dog for a walk and you'll observe something. Dogs notice *everything* ... every bush, every flower and weed, every fire hydrant. Take the same pooch on the same walk as many times as you like, and it's always a new experience for him. Dogs live in the present.

When we practice "dog awareness," we notice that our mind is usually somewhere else. Try eating a meal and tasting every mouthful. Talk to a friend and hear every word. Listen to a song and hear every note. Take a walk and see every tree. Gradually we get better at it.

Affirm to yourself: "I HAVE PLENTY OF TIME." An affirmation, repeated over and over becomes part of our subconscious. When you feel pressed, remind yourself: "I have plenty of time."

The Sufi mystics say that *we are born asleep, we live our lives asleep, and we have to die before we wake up.* I think they are talking about our awareness. So often we are just going through the motions while our mind is out to lunch.

The longer you can stay on the tight rope, the better life gets.

WHY RELAX?

With almost everything we do in life, we are chasing results. But with deep relaxation, meditation or prayer, it's different. You can't chase results. You may know there are long term benefits, but your full attention must be in the present. *The act itself is its own reward.* For once, you are not trying to "get" something—you are *"being"* rather than *"doing."*

When you practice deep relaxation over time, you will notice that the quality of your quiet experience filters into your daily life. You become

more relaxed and more intuitive. It's like dipping a cloth into scented water—each time you do it, a little more of the perfume remains. We all have access to an inner voice—but it is very subtle. When life gets too busy and noisy, we can't hear it. When we quiet what's happening on the outside, we hear the inside. Our intuition is always there, but often we don't listen.

Research continues to confirm that resting your mind is good for your health. In one study, research teams from two world-famous universities studied seventy-three residents in homes for the elderly. Subjects were assigned to either a) no treatment, or b) daily meditation. After four years a quarter of the non meditators had died. All of the meditators were still alive.[3]

In 1978, Robert Keith Wallace completed a ten year study of meditators, evaluating their biological age via three indicators—blood pressure, hearing and near point vision. He found that subjects who had meditated for five years or less were on average five years younger biologically, and that subjects who had meditated more than five years were on average twelve years younger biologically, e.g. sixty year olds had forty-eight year old bodies.

I find that when I take time out to relax, meditate or pray, I feel more balanced and in control. Soon I get complacent and quit my prayer and meditation. Gradually life gets more stressful and I get frustrated. I lose my cool. Then I resume my daily relaxation regimen and life runs more smoothly.

Many busy people go through this cycle. The moral is: *"If you haven't time to relax, you absolutely must do it."* You would think we would learn—but we don't.

Obviously, relaxation gives us a sense of well being, but there are other benefits. *We attract people into our lives who feel much as we do.* When we are feeling peaceful, we attract peaceful people and more peaceful situations. Angry people look at peaceful people and think they are a bit peculiar—so they go looking for fights elsewhere. If you are relatively peaceful, and you do have to deal with angry people, they'll usually follow your lead and behave themselves much better!

If you need help to learn a relaxation or meditation technique, there are plenty of books and groups around that can help you to develop whatever discipline appeals to you.

**"Buy silver, sell gold, book my flight to Frankfurt
and tell Henderson he's fired ... "**

TIPS FOR RELAXING/ MEDITATING:

- HEALING IS A DAILY EVENT. So aim to do it every day and at the same time every day. Early morning is best because you avoid distractions and set yourself up for the day.

- DO IT WHILE SITTING UP—if you lie down, you'll fall asleep.

- IF YOU HAVEN'T GOT TIME TO RELAX, DO IT ANYWAY! Meditation gives you back more time than it takes. See it as "tuning" yourself like you tune a car—twenty minutes each day to improve your efficiency.

AND WHEN PEOPLE ARE HORRIBLE ...

Try this. Every time you get into arguments, have major problems with bosses, husbands, in-laws, pull away. Sit quietly by yourself. Relax. Feel yourself accepting them. Project love to them in whatever imaginative way you choose. If this seems a radical, new age technique for you, try it anyway. Don't try and figure it out—just use it. Many people do. You may be surprised by the results.

IN A NUTSHELL

Start every day with an intention to be balanced and peaceful. Some days you will cruise through until bedtime, and some days you won't make it past breakfast. If peace of mind is your daily goal, you will get better and better.

MATHEWS

GIVE YOURSELF A BREAK!

Have you ever noticed that you can hike all day in the wilderness and feel energized—or spend a morning in a shopping mall, and feel like you've been hit by a truck?

Everything around us has a vibration, be it grass, concrete, plastic or polyester. We pick up the vibrations. Forests and gardens have healing vibrations: they replace our energy. Concrete shopping malls and parking lots have different vibrations: they sap our energy. Cathedrals have elevated vibes. Dirty restaurants with plastic table cloths are low energy places. Smoky bars and strip joints are low energy places—they "strip" your energy.

You don't need to be a genius to realize that your health and feelings are affected by the subtle energies of your environment. When your energy is up, you are resistant to disease and other people's bad moods. When your energy is down, you attract depression and disease.

IN A NUTSHELL

It pays to be selective about where you take your body. It's better to go without than to eat in some restaurants, it's better to stay home than sleep in some hotel rooms. Guard yourself jealously and trust your intuition. Stay out of places that drain you. When a place doesn't feel right, keep walking!

GET SOME SPACE!

It is no coincidence that in cultures the world over, there is a tradition and respect for time alone. During adolescence, the young Native American and African bushman would leave his people and sit on a mountain top or walk the bush, to find his purpose.

The master teachers like Christ, Buddha
and Mohammed all drew inspiration from solitude,
as have the millions of monks, mystics and seekers
who have followed in their footsteps. We each need
a sacred place where the phone doesn't ring, where there's
no newspaper or clock, where we can forget about the bank
balance. Be it a corner of the bedroom, a spot on the balcony
or in a forest, it is our place for contemplation and creation.

THE WHOLE PICTURE

"When we try to pick out anything by itself,
we find it hitched to everything else in the Universe."
John Muir

Since the seventeenth century, science has taken
the (Sir Isaac) Newtonian approach, i.e., if you
want to understand anything, you break it
into pieces, and examine the pieces. If you still
don't understand, break it into smaller bits ...
go from molecules and atoms to electrons,
to quarks and
bozons ... and
eventually
you'll under-
stand the
universe.
Really?

MATTHEWS

"It's for you!"

119

Take a Wordsworth poem and divide it into prepositions and pronouns, then break the words into letters. What more do you understand about the poem? Analyze the "Mona Lisa" into brushstrokes.

Science has done wonders for us, but it's one side of the spectrum. Science dissects. The intellect pulls things apart. The heart brings things together.

There are questions to which information and intelligence have no answers. When you analyze your friends, you lose sight of their beauty. When you analyze and dissect the universe, you separate yourself. When you empathize, you see the larger picture, and you feel closer. Care, and you are instantly connected. Everything in the cosmos is connected. The more we break things down, the more we lose the essentials.

IN A NUTSHELL

The opposite of analysis is synthesis. Health comes from looking at things as a whole—looking at your body as a whole, looking at humanity as a whole.

GRATITUDE AND PEACE OF MIND

"If the only prayer you say in your whole life is 'thank you,' that would suffice."
Meister Eckhart

For a moment, suspend all judgements about your life and the people in it. Imagine you woke up tomorrow morning and said to God, Allah, The Great Spirit, Jehovah, Jim or whatever you like to call the universal power: "Thank you for my life, my family, my home, my friends, my breakfast and thank you for another day." Wouldn't you feel more contented than usual? And before you argue: "But you haven't seen my family," imagine you were able to feel grateful the next day, and the next. Wouldn't you find some extra serenity?

Most of us grow up with feedback that we are not OK. We soon decide that our families, our lovers, our cars and jobs are not OK. We dwell on what's missing. "If only I had some respect at work, if only I had a Mercedes Benz ... " Is it any wonder we find peace of mind so elusive?

Every time we feel thankful for something, we become more peaceful. Every time we say "thank you," we are affirming: "I accept what I have and where I am. I'm learning what I need to learn."

PEACE OF MIND COMES FROM CONCENTRATING ON WHAT YOU HAVE, NOT ON WHAT'S MISSING. When you accept your life, you see how everything in it serves you.

IN A NUTSHELL

If you are serious about peace of mind, at some stage you'll need a sense of gratitude. And here's the crunch—if you want to be grateful, you wake up grateful. If you say: *"When my life gets better, then I'll be grateful,"* you never will be!

AND THEN WHAT?

In a book about finding meaning in life, death deserves a mention. Wouldn't life seem fairer if we never died? Then, at least we could learn from our mistakes! How can you apply all your new-found knowledge— i.e., "that you should avoid buses traveling at high speed," when you've just been hit by one? It would be comforting to have proof that seventy-five years wouldn't see us at the end of the road.

Einstein is encouraging here. Einstein demonstrated that *energy is neither created nor destroyed.* Therefore, when you die, something has to happen to your spirit. Sure, your bones might fertilize the daisies, but there's more to you than bones and gristle. Your spirit must go somewhere!

Out of body experiences also suggest something beyond ... Even if you haven't had an "O.B.E.", you probably know people who have. Aunt Molly tells you: "There I was on the operating table, and suddenly I left my body. I was looking down on my *own* operation. I remember everything the doctors said—and would you believe it, they were talking about the Chicago Bulls?"

You are more than just a body! So what happens to that part of you which isn't "body"?

Einstein and Aunt Molly both give weight to the premise that life goes on. Eastern and Western thinking agree that there is more to learn after we turn up our toes. One thing is certain—while we don't know exactly what is on the other side, death is an incentive to enjoy life while we have it. Quite a clever system, really.

The worst approach you can take is: "I'll suffer in this life but heaven will be my compensation." That's a big chance to take! So much better to say: "Whatever eternity has up it's sleeve, my current goal is to make my life work here and now!"

IN A NUTSHELL

It seems reasonable to assume that any qualities and talents you develop in this life—love, determination, compassion, basket weaving—you'll get to take with you. So our best bet is to develop ourselves to our full potential here and now—and hope the benefits are transferable!

IX

HOW DO YOU
LOVE PEOPLE?
JUST ACCEPT THEM.

Complete acceptance
is unconditional love.

CHAPTER 9

Why Are We Here?
Forgiveness
Family
Love and Fear

WHY ARE WE HERE?

Imagine you came across a competition on your corn flakes packet: *"In ten words or less, answer the question ... 'WHAT IS THE PURPOSE OF LIFE?'"* What would you write?

"Get a freehold house and cram it full of stuff?"

"Make a million and retire to Bermuda?"

"Get my golf handicap down to single figures."

Secretly, each of us knows that there's more to life. We know that PEOPLE COME FIRST—that the BMW's and the Gucci shoes are just trimmings. But sometimes we get side-tracked and the details get the attention—the leather furniture and the new entertainment system.

What is the theme of almost every song and every movie? Caring for people. How often does it take a tragedy to remind us of our real priorities?

Marianne Williamson makes this point when she talks about people on their deathbed. In those final hours, when they are surrounded by their loved ones, how often do people say: "If only I had made an extra twenty grand?" They tend to say things like: "Take good care of your mother, the children ... " They don't often say: "Look after my car." In answer to the question: "Why are we here?" wouldn't it make sense to say: "WE ARE HERE TO LEARN TO LOVE ONE ANOTHER."

Experiments have been carried out in American hospitals where one group of new-born babies are held and stroked for ten minutes, three times a day. The second group aren't stroked. The first group gains weight at twice the rate of the second. Medical science has a long name for this kind of treatment. We don't need scientific words—because we're talking about *love*. The fact is, without love babies don't grow and without love adults suffer exactly the same.

I've lost count of the number of grown men who have said to me at one time or another: "All I wanted my whole life was for my dad to tell me he was proud of me. All I wanted my whole life was for my dad to tell me he loved me."

If we're honest, almost *everything* we do is an attempt to get more love. Everyone you pass on the street, everyone who has ever walked into your office is aching for love and acceptance—and some of us are doing crazy things to get it.

Why even worry about this? Because to make our life really work, we need to know why we are here. If you don't agree that our number one priority is *to love one another*, you may be prompted to clarify what is most important to you, and that's a useful step.

If you do agree, then you can evaluate everything you do by the criteria: *"If I do 'X', will it bring more love into my life, into the lives of my family, friends and neighbors?"*

To love people you don't have to kiss everyone you meet. To love people you don't necessarily have to hand out rice bowls in the Third World. It is judging people less. It is allowing them to wear what they want, live how they want and be who they are without our criticism.

FORGIVENESS

"Forgiveness is the fragrance the violet sheds on the heel that has crushed it."
Mark Twain

Here's what happens. We create rules inside our head for how people should behave. When people break the rules, we resent them. Resenting people for ignoring *our* rules is absurd. Most of us grow up believing that we can punish other people by refusing to forgive them—that is: "If I don't forgive you, *you* suffer." Actually, it's me that suffers. I get the knot in my stomach, I lose the sleep.

Next time you are resenting someone, close your eyes and experience your feelings. Experience your body. Making people guilty makes you miserable.

"How do you live with this creep?"

People do what they do, knowing what they know. Whether you make them guilty makes no difference—except that *it ruins your life*. Things are the way they are. If a hurricane floods your basement, do you say: "I'll never forgive the weather?" If a seagull craps on your head, do you resent the seagull? Then why resent people? We are no more meant to control people than we are meant to control rainstorms and seagulls. The universe doesn't operate on guilt and blame—guilt and blame is just stuff we've made up.

While we're talking about forgiveness, the first step to making your life work is to forgive your parents. Sure they weren't perfect. But when you were a kid, your mom and dad didn't have all the pop psychology books on "successful parenting," and they had a lot of other things to worry about besides raising you! Whatever they got wrong, it is history. Every day that you refuse to forgive your mother is a vote to screw up your life.

PAIN IS INEVITABLE, MISERY IS A CHOICE

You say: "What if someone does something terrible? Do I forgive him?"

I have a friend called Sandy McGregor. In January 1987, a young man with a shotgun walked into his living room and murdered his three teenage daughters. The tragedy saw Sandy descend into a personal hell of pain and anger. Few of us could imagine what he went through.

With time, and the help of friends, he decided that his only chance to make his life work was to let go of the anger, and somehow forgive the offender. Sandy now spends his life helping others to achieve forgiveness and peace of mind. His experience is evidence that it is humanly possible to let go of our resentments, even in the most horrific circumstances. Sandy would also tell you that he let go of his anger for *his own* benefit and *his own* survival.

I notice that people who have had experiences like Sandy fall into roughly two groups. The first group remain prisoners of their own anger and bitterness. The second group achieve an uncommon depth and compassion.

The events that transform us are usually not the things we would choose. As someone said, *we never want to go through what we need to go through to become what we want to become.* Heartbreak, illness, loneliness, desperation … we each get our share. After any major loss, there is always a mourning process. But ultimately, the question is whether the experience makes you harder or softer.

For those of us who are less challenged than Sandy, the choice is the same. *"Do you want your life to work or don't you?"*

DO I *HAVE* TO LOVE (OR AT LEAST LIKE) MYSELF?

Yes! People who don't like themselves are a pain in the neck!

Many people are uncomfortable with the idea of "loving themselves." At the same time, they expect their partners to love them! Isn't that a little odd? To say: *"I couldn't possibly love myself,"* and then get angry with my wife when she doesn't love me? Obviously, to have a healthy relationship, we have to like/love ourselves.

128

We can't give anyone else something that we don't have. We can never accept other people *as they are* until we accept ourselves *as we are*. When we are mesmerized by our own faults, we look for the same faults in other people in the hope it will make us feel better. And we find them, but we don't feel better.

While we concentrate on our own faults, the world will keep punishing us, and we will keep punishing ourselves. We do it with ill health, with poverty, with loneliness. As long as we don't like ourselves, the world won't like us. And then we blame the world.

WHAT DOES IT MEAN TO LOVE MYSELF?

In its simplest form, loving yourself means forgiving yourself. It means admitting that to this point you've lived your life the best way you know how. Stop seeing yourself as guilty. Forget perfection and aim for improvement.

Forgive yourself for your own shortcomings and automatically you begin to let others off the hook for the same things. People reflect back to us what we are. If we pay attention, we are always getting messages, showing us how we need to grow. *The issue is always with ourselves.*

For the sake of our children, we have to accept ourselves. Children follow our example. If you give yourself a hard time, they'll give themselves a hard time—and they'll give you a hard time too!

IN A NUTSHELL

When we forgive ourselves, we stop criticizing other people.

WHAT DOES IT MEAN TO "LOVE THY NEIGHBOR?"

"Love cures two people, the person who gives it and the person who receives it."
Karl Menninger

I believe loving your neighbor means:

- Not judging him
- Not putting labels on him
- Expecting nothing of him

This turns out to be a very practical strategy that can save us a lot of frustration and disappointment. Like most spiritual principles, it is also excellent psychological advice.

We tend to say: "If I understood why Frank is so arrogant, then perhaps I could love the guy." If we make the choice to love Frank, we begin to understand him. Forgiveness and love are one and the same. That's why we find it easier to love babies—because we perceive them as innocent.

Whenever we choose to see love in a situation, we are making progress— mainly because we can't love *and* resent people at the same time!

IN A NUTSHELL

How do you *love* someone? Try substituting the word *"acceptance."* Total acceptance is unconditional love.

MATTHEWS

FAMILY

"WHY DO I HAVE A FAMILY?"

Families were invented to teach us about unconditional love. You can leave your colleagues at the office and your buddies at the bar. But with families it's different. You are stuck with these people who know how to push all your buttons—and you have to learn to love them anyway.

In families, we learn to appreciate people regardless of what they look like or what they can do for us. We learn to love on the inside. In the story *The Velveteen Rabbit*, the Skin Horse seems to be talking about unconditional love:

> *"Real isn't how you are made. It's a thing that happens to you. When a child loves you for a long, long time, not just to play with, but REALLY loves you, then you become Real ... It doesn't happen all at once. You become. It takes a long time. That's why it doesn't often happen to people who break easily, or have sharp edges, or have to be carefully kept. Generally, by the time you are Real, most of your hair has been loved off, and your eyes drop out and you get loose in the joints and very shabby. But these things don't matter at all, because once you are Real you can't be ugly, except to people who don't understand."* [4]

TAKING FAMILY FOR GRANTED

Isn't it funny how we often treat strangers who come to our home for dinner a whole lot better than we treat family? Have you ever entertained strangers? You spend two days setting the table with your best silver and crockery, you serve seafood, strawberries and French champagne—and you never see those people again!

Next week, Mom and Dad come over—and they get leftovers. We are more polite to people we hardly know! Perhaps we should turn it around sometimes—save the lobster for Mom and Dad.

It was only in the last few years of his life that I learned to hug my father. Like many fathers and sons, I quit hugging my dad when I was about eight. I wanted to be "manly." It took me another twenty years to discover that *real* men can show affection.

As an author, I see my face on television and in the newspapers from time to time. I have discovered that Sunday's headline is Monday's garbage.

The question I ask myself is: "What do I mean to those who really know me and rely on me—my family and close friends? Am I dependable, trustworthy, caring and decent?" That's what matters.

SUPPORTING YOUR PARTNER

There are two ways to run a relationship—one is like a team, and the other is like a contest.

Fred is due home at six p.m., and he is already two hours late. Mary is worried sick. "What's happened to my Fred?" At eight-fifteen, Fred walks in the door. On seeing that he is healthy and all in one piece, she screams at him as if to say: "If you are going to come home this late, you could have at least had an accident!"

Fred begins to shout and Mary switches to the dreaded *silent treatment*. Soon they quit talking to each other altogether.

She goes to bed to find a note pinned to her pillow: "I have to be at the office early. Wake me at seven." Fred wakes at nine-thirty to find a note on his pillow: "It's seven o'clock. Wake up!"

So many couples are dedicated to making each other look like idiots.

I can recommend *teamwork*. I am blessed with a partner who spends her life helping and encouraging me. I seek Julie's counsel on every page I write and everything I do. Without her support, I wouldn't be doing what I'm doing. As we grow closer together, it is remarkable how often waiters and flight attendants ask us: "Are you on your honeymoon?" We take that as a huge compliment.

If you have chosen to live together, support each other. If you can't support your partner, it's time to examine why you are in the relationship.

LOVE AND FEAR

"A Course in Miracles" points out that we have two principal states of mind—*love* and *fear*. It suggests that fear is the source of our negative emotions. It's a beautifully simple concept, and a useful starting point for examining our feelings:

Jane says: "If I'm angry, it's anger! It's not fear!" Let's see. Husband Bill arrives home reeking of alcohol and perfume. Jane is very angry. She screams and shouts and hurls plates across the kitchen. Actually, she's screaming because she's *scared*. She's *scared* he doesn't care, *scared* she's losing Bill and *scared* about those long blonde hairs on his sports coat! *When we're angry, we're scared.*

Jim is worried about his mortgage. Jim says: "But when I'm worried, I'm worried." "Worried" is another word for *scared*. How can you worry about something if you have no fear? *When we're worried, we're scared.*

What about jealousy? Jealousy is *fear*. It's thinking you're inferior to other people and fearing they agree with you. *When we're jealous, we're scared.*

Lurking behind anger, jealousy, worry, depression, we always find fear. So how is this love/fear concept useful? It enables us to be more honest with ourselves. We discover that we are usually not upset for the reasons we think.

If I want to eliminate my fears I have to admit they exist. While I'm saying: "You are inconsiderate for making me jealous," I stay stuck. Only when I can ask myself: "Why am I scared when you talk to handsome strangers?" do I begin to be unstuck. Now I recognize *my fears* instead of *your faults*. When I admit my fears, I have a chance to move beyond them.

Admitting our fears helps us to explain our feelings to people we care about:

"Darling the reason I got angry is because I'm scared. I'm scared that if you buy that three thousand dollar outfit, we won't eat for a year."

"I scream at you when you are so late home because I'm terrified that something may have happened to you on the road. If I lost you I don't know what I would do. I get scared."

When we admit our fears, we move away from making other people wrong. In essence, we say: *"I want you to know I'm scared. I'm not saying it's your fault."*

When we accept that we don't have to be perfect any more, and explain our feelings in terms of our fears, our loved ones respond. Admitting vulnerability beats hurling abuse.

Remember also that other people aren't upset for the reasons they think. When they attack you, they are actually scared. Knowing they are scared, you are not so frightened.

You say: "But if love and fear are the two principal emotions, wouldn't that mean many people are scared?" You bet! Lots of people are scared out of their wits—scared of looking silly or looking fat, scared of losing jobs, scared of losing face or losing money, scared of being burgled, scared of growing old, scared of being alone, scared of living and scared of dying. That's why they act so crazy!

What makes them feel better? Being loved.

X

**YOUR MISSION
IN LIFE
IS NOT TO
CHANGE THE WORLD.**

**YOUR MISSION
IS TO
CHANGE YOURSELF.**

**There are no
"outside" solutions,
only "inside" solutions.**

CHAPTER 10

When You Change . . .
You're Not Alone!

WHEN YOU CHANGE . . .

"When you get sick and tired of being sick and tired, you'll change."

Have you noticed that you have days on the freeway when everyone is trying to kill you? Whenever you leave the house angry, it seems people want to run you off the road! When you leave the office feeling irate, people abuse you in the subway. The reverse is also true. How different the world looks when we fall in love!

The world is a mirror—what you feel inside, you get on the outside—which is why YOU CAN'T FIX LIFE BY WORKING ON THE OUTSIDE. If people on the street are unfriendly, changing streets doesn't help! If nobody at work gives you any respect, changing jobs won't fix it.

Most of us learned things inside out! We learned: "If you don't like your job, change it. If you don't like your wife, change her." Sometimes it's appropriate to change your job or your partner. But if you don't change too, you are setting yourself up for more of the same.

Captain Gerald Coffee spent seven years as a prisoner of war in North Vietnam. Reflecting on changes in his attitude, he said: "In the beginning, I would pray to God to change my situation—*God give me the last five minutes prior to my capture, and I'll fly somewhere else ... God, please let the Americans win and get me out of here."*

"As time passed," he said, "my prayers changed ... I began to pray that I might become a better person, that I might not only endure, but even benefit from my experience as a POW." His prayers of "change my *circumstances"* became "change *me.*" He had discovered a fundamental principle, and from that point he began to see some purpose in his condition.

Whatever situation we are in, we are in it because we have lessons to learn from it. *That's why we're there!* Asking God to change our situation makes absolutely no sense. Until we have changed, we still need the situation!

If Mary is struggling in a marriage, *she* has to change. Mary says: "Lord, if you'll just change my husband, Fred, I'll be happy!" Wrong! Fred resents Mary and refuses to change. Mary divorces Fred. Next year Mary is saying: "If you'll just change Chuck ... "

When we say: "God, please change my circumstances and save me the trouble of changing myself," we demonstrate a lack of understanding. The request needs to be: "Change me, change my thoughts about this." As our thoughts about circumstances alter, the circumstances alter.

Does this all seem a bit "new age" and goofy? Look at it in the light of physics. Three hundred years ago Newton proclaimed that all objects have a defined, unchanging reality. But today's Quantum physics, and the Heisenberg uncertainty principle present a different picture, i.e. *The nature of a thing is actually altered by its observer!*

What does this mean to you in your everyday life? That physics confirms what the spiritual masters have always taught—that a thing, a situation is transformed by the observer. As you change your thinking, your life will change. You fixing your life is an *inside* job. You don't need to wait for anyone else to get their act together. When you move the world moves. To the extent that you change, the other players in your life change—or are replaced by new players. While they are helping to teach you your lessons, you are helping to give them theirs.

IN A NUTSHELL

In relationships: WORKING ON YOURSELF WORKS, AND TRYING TO CHANGE OTHER PEOPLE DOESN'T.

THE *WORLD* DOESN'T HAVE TO CHANGE ...

Have you ever been sick in bed, and then ventured outside for the first time in weeks? Isn't it exhilarating just to see sky, trees, even grass? When you meet old friends for the first time in five years, isn't it wonderful? Life is suddenly richer, but not because the world has changed. We have. Joy comes from fresh vision.

Happiness doesn't require that you take something else up, but that you drop something—those thoughts that don't help you. If you go through life taking inventory of people's shortcomings ... "She's too fat, he's got a big nose, she's got a big mouth" it interferes with your peace of mind. Sure, it may give you an illusion of superiority, but you are affirming to yourself that *the world and the people in it are not OK.*

When you choose to accept people, warts and all, you have a whole different feeling about the world and your place in it. It's a great relief.

How do you do it? You have *preferences* about who you spend time with, but you don't make everybody else "wrong." You have preferences about your circumstances but you don't see everything as *right* or *wrong.* You recognize that your ultimate goal is peace of mind, so you decide to see differently.

Fred says: "But my family conditioned me to concentrate on the negative!" Fine. Maturity is that point in our lives when we take responsibility for our thoughts and actions. Now that you are in charge of your mind, Fred, you can change it.

Look for beauty in those around you and you will find more within yourself. YOU SEE PEOPLE NOT AS THEY ARE BUT AS YOU ARE. YOUR EXPERIENCE OF THE WORLD IS ACTUALLY YOU EXPERIENCING YOURSELF. If you don't like what you are seeing, blaming the mirror doesn't help.

IN A NUTSHELL

In fixing your life: WORKING ON YOURSELF WORKS, AND TRYING TO CHANGE THE WORLD DOESN'T.

YOU'RE NOT ALONE!

"When you meet anyone, remember it is a holy encounter. As you see him, you will see yourself. As you treat him, you will treat yourself. Never forget this, for in him, you will find or lose yourself."
A Course in Miracles

The universe is even more miraculous than we may have assumed. It is so exquisitely planned that we are all getting the lessons we need from the other players in our life at any one time.
The spiritual masters taught that we are all one—that your growth is my growth, that your pain is my pain. They taught that on one level, we are all

linked. It's a difficult concept to grasp. But isn't it an explanation for why it is that whenever we change, everybody else changes!

This phenomena of circumstances "coinciding with our needs" was given a name by Carl Jung. He coined the term: *"synchronicity."* He described it as: *"the simultaneous occurrence of two meaningfully but not causally connected events."*

If we accept this idea of *synchronicity:*

- OUR LIFE HAS PURPOSE
- EVERY EVENT AND EVERYONE IN IT HAS A PURPOSE
- WE DON'T FEEL LIKE VICTIMS

Consider it. If you were making a universe, wouldn't you want to give people the opportunity to improve their circumstances by improving themselves, rather than have them all as victims?

You might say: "Well that is a fairly miraculous piece of timing—that six billion people should be always in the right place at the right time to learn their appropriate lessons from each other." Amazing, but perhaps not unlike the way billions of different cells in the human body co-operate.

Of course, there are reasons to resist the idea of synchronicity and our connection to the whole. While we separate ourselves, it's easy to blame people. Once we admit we are connected, we must take more responsibility for ourselves and for others.

But this is what I notice: happy and effective people tend to embrace the concept of "oneness." They see every event in their life as meaningful feedback. They expect circumstances to synchronize in their favor. High performance people discard the idea that life is a lottery.

AM I MAKING CHOICES OR IS MY LIFE PATH ALREADY SEALED?

Where does "predestiny" and "fate" fit into life? Seen from the human perspective, it seems logical that *either* you choose your life direction *or* it has already been laid down. I think both of these things can be happening at the same time—that we are following a path AND we are making our own choices. (Impossible? I think God can arrange that kind of stuff.) One thing we can observe—great people achieve greatness through persistent daily effort. It may be that they had a path to follow, but they didn't wait for someone to carry them down the path.

140

AS WE LEARN MORE ABOUT THE UNIVERSAL LAWS, WE TEND TO MOVE THROUGH THE FOLLOWING PHASES:

Step 1: We have no particular goals. We believe that life is a game of chance. We muddle along going nowhere in particular. This is the victim mentality.

Step 2: We work on our goals. We discover goal setting. We find that visualization and disciplined effort combine to produce extraordinary results. We also discover that sometimes you achieve your goals but they don't make you happier.

Step 3: We work on ourselves. We discover that there is such a thing as doing your best in the present and letting life unfold - that often life will present us with greater rewards than we could ever have imagined. We discover that there is a balance to be achieved between hard work and good timing. We see that there are alternatives to desperation and frustration. As we achieve greater balance and peace of mind, our belief in struggle is replaced by a sense of challenge.

SO WHERE'S THE MEANING?

We don't make our lives meaningful with one great deed. We have to see meaning in lots of little deeds, and find a connection amongst them.

Fred makes his million and asks: "What's it all about?"

Mary scales the corporate ladder and says: "Where's the meaning in all this?"

Sarah has her baby, but she is still depressed.

There's no actual meaning in a million or in being company president or in being a mother. Meaning is in the present. Being "there" is no better than being "here." If you want to find meaning, you pay attention to the moment—and it's in the moment that you find the rewards.

SOURCES

1. "Come from the Heart" Words and Music Susana Clark and Richard Leigh Copyright © 1987 EMI April Music./GSC Music/Lion Hearted Music Inc.
2. BLACK, Dean. 1992, The Frogship Perspective, 1992, Tapestry Communications, p.16-7, 117-8.
3. CHOPRA, Deepak, M.D. 1989, Quantum Healing, Bantam Books, New York, Toronto, p.193-4.
4. WILLIAMS, Margery, 1922, The Velveteen Rabbit, Harper Collins, Sydney, Auckland.

REFERENCES

BARKER, Joel Arthur. 1992, Future Edge, William Morrow and Company, Inc. New York.

CRAWFORD, Roger & BOWKER, Michael. 1989, Playing from the Heart, Prima Publishing and Communications, Rocklin, CA.

DE BONO, Edward. 1985, Tactics, The Art & Science of Success, Fontana/Collins.

JAMPOLSKY, Gerald G., M.D. 1979, Love Is Letting Go of Fear, Celestial Arts, Berkeley, California.

McCORMACK, John with LEGGE, David R. 1990, Self-Made in America, Addison-Wesley Publishing Company, Inc.

MYERS, David G. 1993, The Pursuit of Happiness, Aquarian/Thorsons, Hammersmith, London.

PATENT, Arnold M. 1991, You Can Have It All, Celebration Publishing, Sylva, North Carolina.

RODDICK, Anita. 1992, Body and Soul, Vermilion, London.

SIEGEL, Bernie M.D. Living, Loving & Healing, Aquarian/Thorsons, Hammersmith, London.

WILLIAMS, Marianne. 1992, A Return to Love, HarperCollins, New York.

ZIGLAR, Zig. 1994, Over the Top, Thomas Nelson, Inc., Nashville, Tennessee.

"*FOLLOW YOUR HEART* is a marvel. It is easy to read, full of wonderful stories and guidance tips. I always recommend it to people."

PAUL JOSLYN
President, Life Insurance Association, U.K.

"If success is measured by the positive impact we have on others—and by making the world a better place—you are very successful. I have lost track of how many of your books I have loaned to people over the years—and I've always received positive feedback. I love your books!"

PETER HONSINGER
Kodak, Rochester, New York

"Andrew, *FOLLOW YOUR HEART* helped me enormously in my work and in my life. I have used your techniques in courtroom battles with great success. *FOLLOW YOUR HEART* is inspirational, thought provoking, riveting. I have bought hundreds to share with clients and friends. Everyone should read it."

CHRISTOPHER FERNANDO
Barrister, Kuala Lumpur, Malaysia

"*FOLLOW YOUR HEART* turned my life around ... I literally felt a different person. Thank you for such a wonderful book."

DEBBIE PERSKE
Prosperpine, Australia

"Absolutely fabulous! *FOLLOW YOUR HEART* has changed our lives. It is such cracking and simple advice that everyone should use."

JONATHAN WOOTTON
U.K.

"Thank you Andrew Matthews for writing your latest book that has had such an impact on my life! My husband, who never reads, picked up *FOLLOW YOUR HEART* and could not put it down. He has been quoting you ever since. You are a real inspiration."

DI PADGETT
Montrose, Australia

"I first found *FOLLOW YOUR HEART* in Hong Kong. It is one of the most inspiring books I have ever read—I only wish I had found it twenty years ago! I want to share it with everyone I know, so I am airfreighting fifty copies home to California."

JIMMY KALB
President, Vortex Technologies, San Diego, California.

"*FOLLOW YOUR HEART* is a must read book that I have read over and over. It is so refreshingly simple! It has given me new insights into my relationships with others. Thank you Andrew."

DR. NEIL BAUM
Urologist, New Orleans, Louisiana

"Thank you Mr Matthews for making my life easier. Every time I have problems with my family, colleagues and friends, I always refer to your book."

AZRENE RIZAL
Kuala Lumpur, Malaysia

"Andrew Matthews is the Deepak Chopra for everyday people. He spells it out in simple terms that anyone can understand."

ANDREA HADHAZY
Dix Hills, New York

"Thank you for having the courage to write *FOLLOW YOUR HEART*. I can't tell you how much the lessons within its pages have meant to me ... it is jam packed full of WISDOM. In today's world wisdom is a rare commodity and you bless our country and our world by sharing your wisdom."

AINSLEY PROBST
Newmarket, Australia

"Andrew, *FOLLOW YOUR HEART* has helped change my life for the better. I almost rely on your books as a day to day reference guide now."

LISA THOMPSON
Christchurch, New Zealand

144